God's Wild Herbs

Rita

See you on the path!

And God said, "I give you all these green plants." Gen 1:28&29

God's Wild Herbs

*Identifying and Using 121 Plants
Found in the Wild*

Dennis Ellingson

CLADACH
Publishing

God's Wild Herbs
Identifying and Using 121 Plants Found in the Wild
© 2010 by Dennis Ellingson

Published by CLADACH PUBLISHING Greeley, Colorado 80634
www.cladach.com

Scripture quotations are taken from the Holy Bible, New International Version, NIV. Copyright 1973, 1978, 1984 by International Bible Society. Used by permission of Zondervan Publishing House. All rights reserved.

Recipes on pp. 39, 41, 51, 58, 73, 90, and 93 are reprinted with permission from *The Essential Herbal Magazine,* 1354 N. Strickler Road, Manheim PA 17545 Cover photo by Kit Ellingson. Front cover inset photo by Tina Samms. Interior photo credits on p. 124.

DISCLAIMER: Information in this book is not intended to be taken as a replacement for medical advice. Any person with a condition requiring medical attention should consult a qualified health practitioner or therapist. Furthermore, in identifying wild edible and medicinal plants, the reader is advised to consult several field guides and to seek the advice of local, knowledgable herbalists and outdoorsmen.

Library of Congress Control Number: 2010936403

ISBN-10: 0981892922
ISBN-13: 9780981892924

Printed in the U.S.A.

*To the Master Gardener,
who loves us so much that He gave us so much,
without ceasing, until He gave up His life.*

"*My lover has gone down to his garden, to the bed of spices [herbs], to
browse in the gardens and **gather** lilies.*"
Song of Solomon 6:2 NIV

"*At that time men will see the Son of Man coming in the clouds
with great power and glory. And he will send his angels and **gather**
his elect from the four winds, from the ends of the earth to the ends
of heaven.*"
Mark 13:26-27 NIV

Contents

Guides on the Path 🌿 11
Starting on the Path 🌿 14
Agave, Blue 🌿 17
Alliums 🌿 18
Along the Path ~ Tears 🌿 19
Amaranth 🌿 20
Arrowhead 🌿 20
Arrowleaf Balsamroot 🌿 21
Asparagus 🌿 21
Aspen, Quaking 🌿 22
Bay, California 🌿 23
Along the Path ~ Reminders 🌿 24
Bearberry 🌿 25
Beargrass 🌿 25
Bedstraw 🌿 26
Blueberry, Bilberry, Huckleberry 🌿 26
Brambles: Blackberry, Raspberry 🌿 27-28
Along the Path ~ Thorns 🌿 29
Buffalo Berry 🌿 30
Bunchberry 🌿 30
Burdock 🌿 31
Butternut & Walnut 🌿 31
Cactus 🌿 32-33
Calamus 🌿 34
Cattail, Common 🌿 34
Celery, Wild 🌿 35
Along the Path ~ Bitterness 🌿 36
Chamomile 🌿 37
Cheeseweed 🌿 37
Cherry, Wild & Chokecherry 🌿 38

Chickweed, Common 🌿 39
RECIPE: Chickweed Pesto 🌿 39
Along the Path ~ Self Worth 🌿 40
Chicory 🌿 41
RECIPE: Spinach, Chicory & Mushroom Salad with Bacon Dressing 🌿 41
Along the Path ~ Grumbling 🌿 42
Chiltepin 🌿 43
Clover, Red & White 🌿 43
Clover, Sweet 🌿 44
Coltsfoot, Common 🌿 45
Columbine 🌿 45-46
Comfrey 🌿 46
Cottonwood & Poplar 🌿 47
Cow Parsnip 🌿 47
Crabapple 🌿 48
Cranberry 🌿 48
Creosote or Chaparral 🌿 49
Curly Dock or Yellow Dock 🌿 49
Currant or Gooseberry 🌿 50
Dandelion 🌿 50-51
RECIPE: Dandelion Jelly 🌿 51
Daylily 🌿 52
Along the Path ~ Don't Worry 🌿 53
Elderberry 🌿 54
False Solomon's Seal 🌿 54-55
Fern 🌿 55
Fireweed 🌿 56
Flax 🌿 56
Along the Path ~ Christ's Blood 🌿 57

Ginger ~ 58
RECIPE: Wild Ginger Dip ~ 58
Grape ~ 59
Ground Cherry ~ 59
Groundnut ~ 60
Hackberry ~ 60
Hawthorn ~ 61
Hazelnut ~ 61
Hickory & Mockernut ~ 62
Horseradish ~ 62
Horsetail ~ 63
Ironwood, Desert ~ 64
Jojoba ~ 64
Juneberry or Serviceberry ~ 65
Juniper ~ 66
Along the Path ~ Idolatry ~ 67
Labrador Tea ~ 68
Lamb's Quarters ~ 68
Lettuce ~ 69
Lily, Yellow Pond ~ 69
Lotus ~ 70
Lovage ~ 70
Madrone ~ 71
Maple, Oregon Broad-leaf ~ 71-72
Mesquite ~ 72
Along the Path ~ Joy of the Lord ~ 73
Milkthistle ~ 74
Milkweed ~ 74-75
Miner's lettuce ~ 75
Mint (Bergamot, Peppermint, Pennyroyal, Spearmint) ~ 76
Along the Path ~ Prosperity ~ 77
Mormon Tea ~ 78
Mountain Ash, American ~ 78
Mulberry ~ 79

Mullein ~ 79-80
Along the Path ~ Promises & Power ~ 81
Nettle ~ 82
New Jersey Tea ~ 83
Oak ~ 83
Ocean Plants ~ 84
Along the Path ~ Obedience ~ 85
Ocotillo ~ 86
Paloverde ~ 86-87
Passionflower ~ 87
Pawpaw ~ 88
Pecan ~ 88
Pennycress ~ 89
Peppergrass ~ 89
Persimmon ~ 90
RECIPE: Persimmon Cookies ~ 90
Along the Path ~ Hospitality ~ 91
Pickerelweed ~ 92
Pine, Pinyon ~ 92
Plantain ~ 93
RECIPE: Wild Plantain Cookies ~ 93
Purslane ~ 94
Redwood ~ 94
Sagebrush ~ 95
Along the Path ~ Paying the Price ~ 96
Saint-John's Wort ~ 97
Salal ~ 99
Salsify ~ 99
Sassafras ~ 100
Sea Grape ~ 100
Shepherd's Purse ~ 101
Sorrel ~ 101
Spruce ~ 102
Sunflower & Jerusalem Artichoke ~ 103
Along the Path ~ Christ in the Trinity ~ 104

Sweet Gale ~ 105
Tumbleweed ~ 105
Watercress ~ 106
Wild Basil ~ 106
Wild Carrot or Queen Anne's Lace ~ 107
Wild Mustard ~ 107
Along the Path ~ Faith ~ 108
Wild Oregon Grape ~ 109
Wild Plum & Wild Pacific Plum ~ 109-110
Wild Rose ~ 110
Wild Strawberry ~ 111
Willow ~ 111
Along the Path ~ A Place of Weeping ~ 112
Witch Hazel ~ 113
Wolfberry ~ 113-114
Wood Sorrel ~ 114
Yarrow ~ 115
Yerba Buena ~ 115-116
Yucca ~ 116
Staying on the Path ~ Conclusion ~ *117*
Friends on the Path ~ 118
Photo Credits ~ 124
Sources ~ 126
Acknowledgments ~ 127
About the Author ~ 128

~ Publisher's Foreword ~

Guides on the Path

"Anyone who understands nature as God's creation sees in nature, not merely God's 'works', but also 'traces of God', ciphers and hidden tokens of his presence."
—Jürgen Moltmann in *God In Creation*

In this day of garage sales and eBay® you've heard the expression, "One man's junk is another man's treasure." Well, as the "Herb Guy" Dennis Ellingson illustrates, you could also say, "One man's weed is another man's herb."

Take dandelions, for instance. After a long, snowy winter, yellow dandelion flowers splashed across a grassy lakeside are pretty and perky harbingers of spring. But when they poke their heads up in your greening lawn, then quickly go to seed for spring winds to spread, it's time for battle. Read this book, though, and you might look at dandelions differently next spring. Rather than spraying poison, take them as a gift of fresh, healthful salad greens that you haven't had to plant—just pull them and eat them!

God has given healthful gifts to us in nature, and we don't always recognize them. Past generations and native peoples have learned and utilized these benefits. Europeans brought old world plants, seeds, and herb lore. Native American Indians had long known what the mountain men, frontiersmen, and homesteaders began to learn from the land and its flora. Often, their use of wild plants was a matter of survival.

Over a century ago my great-grandparents came in covered wagon to the eastern Colorado plains as homesteaders. Great-Grandma Flora Belle used to speak affectionately of her calendulas. The bright orange flowers would be a mood lifter when spring finally came to the prairie. Calendulas were called "pot herbs" because they were cooked and eaten, offering both flavor and nutrition. Now we sometimes add the flowers to salads for chic color. But to my Scottish and English great-grandparents, making a living at dry farming, calendulas were part of their story of physical and emotional survival. I remember Grandma's delicious spiced crabapples. In her ancient, dog-eared cookbook I found recipes for mint jelly, pickled nasturtium seeds, watercress soup, pickled plums and spiced currants. Many of these fruits and herbs she could forage in the wild.

My other grandmother was part Cherokee Indian—a naturally beautiful and graceful woman, who was close to nature and nature's God. My grandfather, a farmer-turned-preacher, hoed straight rows and pulled errant plants. But Grandma tried to protect the "volunteers" wherever they chose to break through the soil in response to water and sun. She nurtured them as lovingly as she did neighborhood children. One time we found fennel growing wild along the drive to their rural, hilltop home. When I recognized it, picked some and chewed it to enjoy the licorice flavor, Grandma smiled approvingly.

As kids, my sister and I explored vacant lots, alleys, and backwoods places in rural California. When we came upon wild blackberries, plums, crabapples, or old, forgotten walnut, fig or pomegranate trees, we'd eat our fill, sometimes wincing from the sourness, but delighted in our secret find, oblivious to the juice stains on our faces and clothes. We would chew on clover leaves (and make chains with the flowers) and suck the nectar from honeysuckle. I admit, we also had to pull stickers out of our flimsy flipflops (and the paws of our faithful little dog who followed us everywhere). And many times we contracted the miserable, itchy rash of poison oak.

I don't know whether I ever asked Grandma, "Why did God create weeds?" But I imagine she would have looked at me with her piercing gray eyes and in her typical cryptic way, ask in return: "Did he?" She often gave me thoughts to chew on. From her I learned to look at things from different angles and to respect all living things.

I believe respect is the key, when it comes to our relationship to the Creator and to his creation. We respect what the Bible says about God and creation, that "in the beginning God created the heavens and the earth," and that he declared his creation "good." That "every good and perfect gift comes down from the father of lights, with whom there is no shadow of turning." That "through him all things were made and in him all things hold together." That God so loved the world that he sent his only Son to live in human skin, to be susceptible to mosquito bites, poison oak and piercing thorns.

Jesus walked from town to town on foot paths. He observed the natural world around him and gleaned from it object lessons as he taught his followers. He said, "Look at the birds of the air" and "Consider the lilies of the field." . . . *Look!* . . . *Consider!*

If we look at and consider wild fauna and flora they will speak to us of his continuing presence and influence. As Dennis Ellingson shares in this book, we see the threeness of the clover leaves (as recognized by Irish Celts), the sacred symbolism of the passion-flower (as utilized by early Spanish missionaries to the new world), the "red blood" of St John's wort.

My guides on this herb-foraging path (and publishing vision) are my grandmothers (and you have your own influencers); Jesus (who walks with us and teaches us on life's upward path); and Dennis Ellingson, whose first book, *God's Healing Herbs,* has brought helpful information and inspiration to thousands of gardeners and health-conscious readers. In this companion volume Dennis takes us out of our cultivated gardens—into the wilds of forest, pasture, pond and meadow. Wild plants grow everywhere, and you can find them.

It's good to know, if the time came that we couldn't get food as easily as we do now, that we could survive by using the edible wild plants around us. I hope that necessity never comes; but the knowledge to be able to go out and forage for wild food does give a certain confidence and satisfaction.

Herbal medicinals have grown in popularity and use. Many herbs, whether wild or cultivated, are being scientifically studied and prepared in liquid or capsule form. You can go to the store and buy them.

I used to work in my yard or garden, or take walks on the trail by the river, and recognize a few wild plants or "weeds" that I knew were edible, such as sunflowers, dandelions, and wild rosehips. But most of the green, flowering things that sprang up in summer were a wild bunch of strangers to me.

Now, since preparing this book for publication, I'm taking walks on the same familiar paths, but recognizing individuals in the crowds of summer greenery. First, it takes looking. Then considering. Then touching, smelling, and perhaps tasting. Now on my walks I'm noticing wild asparagus, mullein, wild mint, Jerusalem artichoke, milkweed, ground cherries and purslane. This summer I tried cooking and eating young tumbleweed; snacking on wild Oregon grapes; adding dandelion greens to a salad. I'm not sure I'll make a habit of eating tumbleweed; but wild berries will always be a treat. Just as important to me as the food value, though, is that the plants are becoming friends whose names I know and with whom I'm familiar.

So, when walking across your yard or city park, through a mountain meadow or forest, on a windswept sea cliff, or along a sunny country road, take this book with you. And I challenge you, dear reader, to find your own answer to the question, "Is this plant a weed or is it an herb?" At the very least, ask yourself, "In getting to know these wild plants, and observing them, perhaps wisely using them, might I open my life to better appreciate all of creation . . . and to experience more of their Creator (and mine)?"

~ Catherine Lawton, Cladach Publishing
   Colorado, August 2010

~ Author's Introduction ~
Starting On the Path

Just an hour's drive from our home my wife, Kit, and I took a recent outing into the Cascade Mountains of the Pacific Northwest. We took a little time to walk along the Pacific Crest Trail in the Southern Oregon section below Mt. McLaughlin. It was midsummer, and we were pleasantly surprised at how many wild herbs and flowers we noticed in just that short hike of a mile and half round trip.

Within a few minutes we identified Pennyroyal, two varieties of Blackberry, Wild Strawberry, Wild Red Columbine, Tiger Lily, Wild Pink Roses, Bleeding Heart, and Wild Oregon Grape, just to name a few. This year around home we have found plenty of Brook Mint along the river banks plus Chamomile, Yellow Balsam Root, Wild Pacific Plums, and Currants. We didn't have to travel far to find Elderberry trees full of blossoms, Mallow, Mullein, Blue Flax, and California Poppy. The list could go on and on.

We feel greatly blessed to live in the Northwest of the U.S., and we have visited many other places over the years. During the winters we spend time in Arizona where we enjoy discovering many native and useful plants, such as the Agave for its sweet nectar. There we find Mesquite and Prickly Pear offering many nutritional and medicinal benefits.

Wherever you live, whatever your neck of the woods, we imagine you could find an abundance of native and naturalized plants. This makes for a great outing in identifying and gathering God's wild herbs. What a wonderful experience the Creator has waiting for you.

That is what this book is about. It is also meant to be a companion volume to my book, *God's Healing Herbs*. The two books complement each other. You may find these to be indispensable to your library if you are "into" herbs. *GHH* is meant to get you out of doors, into your yard and growing herbs that you can use every day. Now *GWH* will get you outside the fence, past the city limits and beyond—where you can locate, identify, gather, use, and enjoy the incredible abundance that God has provided. These wild plants can contribute to a healthier and heartier life.

The premise remains the same as for the preceding books: We seek to follow and enjoy what God has prescribed and provided for us.

"Then God said, 'I give you every seed-bearing plant [herb] on the face of the whole earth and every tree that has fruit with seed in it. They will be yours for food. And to all the beasts of the earth and all the birds of the air and all the creatures that move on the ground—everything that has the breath of life in it—I give every green plant for food.' And it was so." (Gen. 1:29-30)

When God said "every green plant" he created and provided much. Estimates are that there are 350,000 individual plant types that currently grow on our planet. Of those 350,000 estimated plants growing today about two thirds have been identified.

I want to share with you what my wife and I are discovering—the enjoyment of what God has provided—especially all those plants (I am both a Bible geek and a plant geek). Included here are listings of wild herbs in various areas of the U.S. The number of plant species is staggering and I could spend a life time learning and writing about them and still only scratch the surface.

So my goal is to provide you with a field guide meant to be studied first and then taken with you to find the plants that will be the most identifiable and locatable for you. We will do this methodically as would a good investigative reporter. We will identify *what* the plant is, *where* you will find it, *why* to harvest it, *when* to harvest and use it, and *how* to use it.

Like every other book I have written, I hope it inspires you to get to know better the God of all creation and the Savior of our souls.

What exactly is an herb? There are many definitions. The Hebrew word *Lachanon* is a word for garden plants that have a medicinal or culinary value. This is indicated by author W. E. Shewell-Cooper in his classic book, *Plants, Flowers and Herbs of the Bible*. In *The Revell Concise Bible Dictionary* herbs are defined as small plants used to flavor food or for their odor or medicinal use.

Genesis 1:28-30 seems to indicate that all plant life is an herb as stated in that edict by God himself. I have come to the conclusion that all plant life is an herb or has herbal benefits. We still do not know what all the plants can provide. Some, such as tobacco and marijuana, are used for wrong purposes. Numerous plants can be absolutely deadly if used in the incorrect way. Nonetheless, there seems to be enough evidence that all plants, in one form or another and in one way or another, can have herbal value.

Wild crafting is the term for identifying, gathering or foraging and using the edible and/or medicinal parts of wild plants. While gathering, one should follow a protocol. If you plan on some serious gathering, then it would behoove you to make sure you know what your state and county laws may say about it. Some plants are just illegal to gather and some require permits. To find out what and how much is legal to gather, go to your state's official web site. All states have state flowers and most have state trees. Some states have even adopted specific herbs as a state symbol. These may have protected status.

How much should you take when harvesting? The rule of thumb is no more than one third of the plant, if possible. It is best to gather in the morning or in the early evening so the plant can more easily bear the shock.

Most geographic areas of the U.S. have local connoisseurs of the wild things. Often times these folks conduct talks and walks. If you have never done any gathering or wild crafting then going with a knowledgeable person first is a great idea. He or she will know where to go, what not to pick and what to do with what is foraged.

Unique to this type of book but typical of my herb books, we provide devotions or meditations. These thoughts are my own as I contemplate creation and the Creator. These thoughts are for you to consider when walking along the path. May they help you draw on, not just the natural, physical, and emotional senses you feel, but the spiritual ones as well. After all, we are physical, emotional, and spiritual beings. God created us that way.

As I thought of the title for these devotions, "Along the Path," I was reminded of the verse that talks about a Christian's journey. It is not necessarily on a wide and easy road always laid out smooth and clear before you; "but small is the gate and narrow the road that leads to life" (Matthew 7:14). May these little thoughts help you start and stay on the path that leads to life everlasting.

~ Dennis Ellingson
  Oregon, March 2010

The Wild Herbs

Agave, Blue (Mahonia trifoliate): Nectar is gathered from the big "century plants" or Blue Agave. In recent years I enjoy this wonderful sweetener with a very subtle taste. A great alternative to sugar and other sweeteners. If you are trying to get away from cane sugar and corn syrup but don't care for honey, then agave nectar may be for you. We have used it for many purposes in baking, hot breakfast cereals, beverage sweeteners, jams and jellies. Unlike honey, agave nectar doesn't crystallize in your pantry in a short while.

Traditionally used to make tequila, a healthful sweetener seems a better use. Agave is a common sight in deserts of the Southwest and Colorado. It also makes a unique garden plant in milder areas, and it is quite hardy. Agave is a succulent with big fleshy upright leaves with spines that will be happy to snag you and difficult to get out. There are numerous varieties of the plant. Blue agave has been called the century plant because of its long life. At the end of its life span the plant shoots up a long spiky flower that may grow to 10 feet tall. This stalk is amazingly heavy and will eventually topple the plant, exposing the roots and the plant will die.

Parts used: The root is used as a body cleanser and hair wash. The nectar is commercially gathered from the core of a plant that is at least 7 years old. Tea from the dried leaves is a stomach tonic. The flower stalk and leaves are ground for flour.

Caution: The leaves of the agave must be cooked or dried; they are considered poisonous if consumed fresh. To try using agave, I strongly suggest you find a local expert who knows the proper process. For people who are diabetic or hypoglycemic this may or may not be a good alternative. Before using agave check with your healthcare provider.

Alliums, Field Garlic (A. vineale) Wild Garlic (A. canadense), Wild Leeks aka Ramps (A. tricoccum), Wild Onion, (A. stellatum) Nodding Wild Onion (A. cernuum): These staples of our kitchen pantry can be found growing in many places, often in abundance. Sometimes all you need to do is follow your nose. Found by spotting the straight grass-like stems and the flowers that bloom from late spring to early fall, depending on variety and location.

Wild garlic and wild onion can grow to 2 feet tall. Pinkish flowers may grow in a great flower head similar to garden onion. In some varieties it is a more drooping flower head with fewer flowers. Leeks grow to nearly 2 feet with a clustered head of flowers that look like a child's drawing of a star. A number of other plants out there look like these, such as poison hemlock and death camas. The distinction is in the smell. If it doesn't have that pungent onion smell, then stay away from it. These native plants grow pretty much everywhere, preferring rich soils. There are perhaps a thousand varieties of alliums, including a number of summer annuals for the flower garden.

Parts used: All parts of the plant are used in the same way you would use commercially- or home-grown alliums.

Some consider onions a "super food"; new research indicates that consuming the onion family helps ward off cancer. Two of the compounds found in alliums that seem to be of the best benefit are sulfur and quercetin. They are powerful antioxidants helping to minimize the development of free radicals in many parts of the body. These pungent wonders are very helpful in keeping cholesterol and triglyceride levels in the safe zone. They also may help with atherosclerosis, colds, asthma, bronchitis and on and on. I don't know about you; but after learning all this, I may not exactly know what I am having for dinner tonight, but it will include onions or garlic or both.

Wild Garlic

Wild Onion flowers

Wild Garlic flowers

Along the Path

Who has not shed tears while cutting up an onion? And don't rub your eyes; that only makes it worse. You probably remember the story of the Exodus as the Israelites left for the Promised Land. Their grumbling and disobedience caused them to be punished by marching through the desert for forty years and never arriving to enjoy God's promise. Even though God supplied their every need the scripture says that they "started wailing and said, 'If only we had meat to eat! We remember the fish we ate in Egypt at no cost—also the cucumbers, melons, leeks, onions and garlic.'" (Numbers 11:5)

"What a thing to cry over," we might think. In fact it reminds me of what an exasperated parent might say to a petulant and disobedient child: "Don't you cry, or I will give you something to cry about!"

Tears, of course, are a part of each of our lives. We shed more tears over pain, sadness and suffering than joy it seems. If we read our Bible in Revelation it states that God will wipe away every tear and we will never shed another tear again. This is indeed something to look forward to, especially during a time of sadness when the tears flow too easily.

What about the tears of God? Does he cry? In Gethsemane, before Jesus's arrest, he has gone to pray. He was in such agony that it was as if he shed blood from his very pores. We can not begin to understand what it meant for him to die for us, but if the all-powerful God could be overwhelmed, then this must have been the closest he came to that.

In our limited measure of understanding and with all the horror that goes on in the world, one might begin to think that somehow God is dispassionate and uncaring for those who suffer.

The story of the raising of Lazarus tells us differently. You can read it for yourself in John Chapter Eleven. What we see is the Lord Jesus "deeply moved and troubled" over his friend's death. Yet he knows how it will turn out, that he will raise Lazarus from death to life and give him back to his sisters. Still he was deeply moved and troubled. This wasn't the impotent feeling we may experience when we are saddened by the plight of another, but find ourselves knowing not what to say or do. This was a greater love. Even though he could solve the tragedy with the snap of his fingers, he was deeply moved and troubled. He is not immune to our suffering and suffers along with us. Jesus is the Suffering Servant, one who cries when we cry.

Amaranth aka Pig Weed and many other names. (Amaranthus retroflexus, A. palmeri): A tall spiky flower with numerous varieties. Those available in North America display spear shaped stalks with an abundance of green, then red, then dark pink flower pods as it matures. The oval leaves are dull green. The plant grows abundantly in the East and Midwest. The desert South has A. palmeri.

Parts used: Tender leaves and shoots, added to salads or boiled. They have a spinach taste. Medicinally, amaranth is a lower tract digestive aid. Seeds, utilized by people in the South and Mexico, are ground and used as flour. There is much interest in amaranth because of the seed's nutritious possibilities in that its protein value is higher than wheat and it is gluten free. Like oats, amaranth can help with the control of cholesterol and high blood pressure.

You can purchase amaranth seed and flour in health food stores and online. The gathering of the seeds at the end of this plant's short life is a challenge because the flower heads are covered in stickers that can be quite irritating. The seeds are shaken out and may number in the thousands.

Arrowhead or Wapatoo (Sagattaria latifolia) also Grass-leaved Arrowhead (S. graminea) and Sessile Fruited Arrowhead (S. rigida): This is an aquatic plant that you may find around ponds, streams, wetlands and even in such places as irrigation ditches. I recently spotted a ditch full of them near Tulelake in Northern California. Also known as "duck potatoes," because the part harvested is the tuber, which has a taste and appearance similar to potato. Digging them, however, is quite different. Most people who go after them, soon realize that there is no way to stay dry in the process. The leaves are very prominent and look like arrows with the points growing up. This is a lush green plant that will grow abundantly with enough water.

Arrowhead is widespread, growing nearly everywhere in the country. An important staple for Native Americans. Assumedly, they introduced it to the European pioneers.

Parts used: The tuber can be used and cooked like a potato. In his book, Euell Gibbons describes using arrowhead to make something similar to a traditional potato salad.

Arrowleaf Balsamroot (Balsamorhiza sagittata): One of my all-time favorite wildflowers. As I'm writing this, I cannot remember a spring when I've seen more of them. They fill the hills around the Columbia Gorge, east of the Cascades and are plentiful in our area of Southeastern Oregon.

A big showy plant with a pungent odor. The large yellow flowers look like sunflowers but bloom long before native and garden varieties of sunflower have even given it consideration. The pale green, broad leaves resemble large arrow points.

Predominantly, but not exclusively, high desert plants of the Great Basin. They are found through the Sierras and stretching on the east side of the slope nearly to Death Valley. Found in Nevada, Idaho, Utah, into the Rockies way up into Canada. These are sun loving plants; you will find them in most abundance in those locales.

Parts used: Leaves and roots, gathered in spring when they contain the most moisture. Medicinally the main use of this plant is to treat colds, sore throats, and such.

Topically the leaves are used to treat burns, sores, and similar conditions from head to toe. It helps with scalp disorders and fungal infections. As a food source, the seeds can be dried, roasted, and added to your favorite baked goods.

Asparagus (Asparagus officinalis): If memory serves, this plant was my first encounter with taking something to eat from the wild. During summers my sister and I would stay a week or two with our grandparents, on both sides. Both sets of grandparents grew huge gardens because they lived in a time when that is what you did. They all did gardening very well. After one of my grandmothers had picked peas and beans she would head out to an irrigation ditch near the farm. It was one channel in a large system that helped farmers irrigate what otherwise was an arid land. One day I went with her.

She brought a knife and basket and soon she was in the watery ditch searching out fresh young spears of asparagus. I don't recall whether I had eaten it before but I remember that I thought it tasted great, and it didn't come from a garden or a grocery store.

No one has made the idea of stalking the wild asparagus more famous than has Euell Gibbons. He sparked a whole generation to go back to nature to gather the wild foods.

Wild asparagus is considered a garden escapee, with the help of birds. It is found in most places of the U.S. In the spring

and early summer the plant shoots up dark green spears from underneath the ground. This is how you know the plant is there. From that a fern-like stalk appears, which will last all season before dying off. The bulk of the plant is the rhizomes hidden underground.

Start looking in ditches and other wet places not far from civilization. Because it is a garden escapee, it is less likely that you would find it in a wilderness setting. You want to search for something that looks and smells exactly like asparagus. I have often looked at horsetail and thought it could be confused with asparagus. There is no difference between wild asparagus and that cultivated in a garden.

Parts used: The spears. Asparagus is one of those unique and wonderful plants that is as much beneficial herb as delectable vegetable. It has a pleasing, unique taste and texture. It is a natural diuretic and considered a good urinary and bladder tonic. If you have eaten it, the next time you need to urinate, you will notice the strong smell. I believe that is a sign that the herbal benefits are working. It helps not only to clean out the kidney system, but also to lower dangerous blood pressure. High in fiber, it will help to keep your digestive tract regular. The only problem with asparagus is that it has a short season, mostly spring and early summer.

Asparagus may be boiled, sauteed or grilled. Some people eat it raw. It freezes well.

Aspen, Quaking (Populus tremuloides, see also Poplar): Without a doubt this is my favorite tree of the Great Basin lands. Although its range is through much of New England, through the Great Lakes region, into the Rockies and the high desert lands of the West and into Northern Arizona and New Mexico, the tree grows much more in Canada and Alaska than in the U.S. I am fascinated by the beautiful white bark, the heart shaped leaves with their red stems that quake or tremble at the slightest breeze. Come fall, the golden leaves bring honor to autumn in the high desert which looks dry and barren at that time of year. The trees grow in groves or colonies by sending out suckers. These trees are sun lovers and don't do well in shady areas. If you want aspen in your yard, you will only need to plant one. Place it where you won't mind the suckers that rapidly turn into trees. A fast growing tree with plentiful water. We have seen giants along rivers, lakes and meadow areas.

Parts used: Leaves and bark. Aspen can be both edible and a medicinal. The buds can be

Aspen Trees, above: summer foliage, below: fall foliage

made into a tea or syrup. Some people eat the buds right off the tree as a snack or consume the soft inner bark. A salve from the buds has been used for skin irritations, muscle aches and pains, and even skin cancer. Gathered before they blossom, the buds plus the bark, gathered in the fall, are commonly used as a tonic for digestive distress, as a diuretic, for fevers and even prostate infections.

Tea from the bark is made by using one ounce of bark per one quart of water that has just cooled down from a rolling boil.

Bay, California, aka Oregon Myrtle or California Laurel (Umbellularia californica): This is a uniquely handsome tree. Broad spreading with oblong, oval evergreen leaves. The flowers are small clusters of white in the spring. From the flowers fruit forms into oval shaped violet berries. The tree is found in the southwestern forests of Oregon and throughout much of coastal California. The tree is also called the headache tree by those who have received healing or adverse effects from crushing the leaves to smell them. It will either take away a headache, even migraines, or it will give you one. According to *The Tree Book,* the vapor emitted from the crushing of the leaves is toxic. Depending on habitat and climate the tree may grow as a large shrub to a fairly tall tree reaching up to 100 feet. Standing under one gives you the sense of being under an umbrella. The tree often grows as wide as it does tall. It is related to the sassafras tree which grows in the eastern U.S.

Parts used: Leaves. Essential oils are extracted from the leaves for medicinal use.

Like many other herbs, the tea is a digestive aid that gives a warming and calming effect. As a topical, the leaves crushed, or the oil extracted, are used to treat rheumatism and bruises. It also acts as an astringent for skin irritants and even dandruff. Dried leaves are used for culinary purposes. This is a strong herb, so a little goes a long way.

Bay (Oregon Myrtle) wood is used for lumber and beautiful works of art.

California Laurel

California Bay

Oregon Myrtle

Along the Path

In the Bible, the bay tree's few mentions are also as the green tree, specifically referring to its evergreen leaves. For a time we lived in an area that was abundant with bay trees. I especially liked looking at them in the winter. In the drab grays and browns of winter, these trees would look healthy and stately as if able to withstand the harsh seasons.

The following is a reminder to us that God is the tree's Creator too: "All the trees of the field will know that I the Lord bring down the tall trees and make the low tree grow tall. I make dry the green tree and make the dry tree flourish." (Ezekiel 17:24) It is a good reminder of who is in charge and of the caring nature of God, the Creator. If you are on the trail, look up, see the splendid trees. Let these majestic beauties be a reminder of our infinitely more majestic Creator.

Bearberry, Kinnikinik or Uva Usa (Arctostaphylos uva ursi): This is a plant with numerous names, a member of the manzanita family. This plant is distinguished from the upright manzanita tree which can grow to 8 feet tall. Bearberry is a more prostrate vine type. Bearberry grows in much of the country, but more in the northern states and into Canada.

Leaves are leathery, green, shiny; bark is reddish, rough. In the spring to summer the plant produces beautiful small pinkish flowers growing in clusters like a bunch of pink bells. When they are in bloom, bees and other nectar gathering insects are in abundance. From this comes the berry, a favorite of local bears. The natives knew it as kinnikinik.

Parts used: The fruit is consumed as food. You can eat them fresh, but they taste better cooked. You can make jam or jellies from them in a similar way that you

would use currants. The leaves have a more medicinal effect. In limited amounts, bearberry leaves help with urinary tract concerns, but too much could actually irritate the situation. It is only a short term medicinal. It is also considered a heart tonic like hawthorn. Also said to be helpful for men suffering with benign prostate hyperplasia.

Beargrass (Nolina microcarpa) or (Xerophyllum tenax): The plant protrudes long spear-like leaves. From the center tall shoots rise to 5 feet. These have a large flower head, feathery in appearance. It is part of the lily family; but if you get too close, it's a lily with an attitude.

Beargrass grows mostly in the West, from north to south and east to the Rockies. There are questions about the name's origin. First thought is that bears eat it. Second thought is that if you grab one of the leaves you may feel like you've been mauled by a bear; its razor sharp edges will shred you.

Parts used: The fibrous leaves, dried and split, used in weaving very durable baskets. The young stalks are roasted. The buds and flowers can be eaten fresh. Seeds of the plant have been ground and used to make flour. The roots have been dried and pounded into powder to make teas.

Bedstraw aka Cleavers; also Goosegrass, (Galium aparine), Northern Bedstraw (Galium boreale), Oregon Bedstraw (G. oreganum) Intermountain Bedstraw: (G. serpenticum) Yellow Bedstraw (G. vernum): Drink your bedstraw, don't sleep on it. This plant is related to the coffee plant. Most distinguished by whorls of slim leaves and clustered, white or yellow, tiny flowers. The plant grows in height from ½ to 2½ feet tall. An annual. Numerous varieties grow all over the U.S.

Parts used: The whole plant, except yellow bedstraw. The seeds are used to make a coffee-like beverage. The bristled fruit or seeds are slow roasted and ground just like one would coffee beans. Cleavers seed lovers think this is better than coffee. This beverage is a general digestive and urinary tract tonic. Also used to treat upper respiratory complaints. Young shoots cook up nicely as greens.

Blueberry, Bilberry & Huckleberry (Vaccinium species): Grows in much of the East; abundant in the state of Maine. All varieties grow in much of the Northwest, through western Canada and Alaska; especially west of the Cascades, in the Cascades and in the rainy areas of the West. Blueberries, bilberries (a smaller wilder berry) and blue, black and reddish huckleberries grow and prosper abundantly in these places. You just have to beat the forest animals to them.

You will find these wonderful morsels in shaded, moist areas. These plants tend to be under-story plants that prefer to grow under trees for shade and protection. True blueberries are the largest of the species. The plant can grow 4 to 5 feet tall. Bilberry and huckleberry plants are usually smaller. Flowers bloom mid spring and berries come on early summer to early fall.

Alaskan huckleberry, a small, blue to black round berry, grows in the Northwest in the Cascades Mountain Range from about Roseburg, Oregon on up. We found this species in abundance near Pacific City, Oregon, in November, just before Thanksgiving. We found enough to make a wonderful huckleberry pie as part of our Thanksgiving abundance. Blueberries grow the whole length of the Cascades. Black huckleberries grow throughout the Cascades, the Coast Range, around the mountains of Northeast Washington and down into the Wallowa Mountains and Hells Canyon into Oregon. California huckleberries grow in the Coast Range from Northern California through Washington. We like to pick in Oregon, around Mt. Adams, in the Rogue-Umpqua divide above Union Creek and the aptly named Huckleberry Mountain near the southwestern border of Crater Lake National Park. We also like to stop at a restaurant in Union Creek that bakes great huckleberry pies!

Parts used: Obviously the berry, but also the leaf. Blueberries, etc. have been touted in recent days as the new miracle or super food and there seems to be good reason. The berries are high in antioxidants. Interestingly enough, the leaves used as a tea, have an effect similar to cranberries in helping to treat and correct urinary tract issues. Look for younger, unblemished leaves. Dry in a cool, dry place out of direct sunlight. These berries are being used for helping to regulate blood sugar levels in people with diabetes. The only negative I have heard is that people who are hypoglycemic and eat too many berries, and nothing else, can have an adverse reaction. Research is being done on the benefit this family of berries has for eyes. May improve night vision and help with eye strain. I have heard that if you are feeling a little anxious, have some berries. They may help stabilize your mood.

Think about all those huckleberry pies, blueberry muffins, jams and teas. Man, oh man, the list goes on. Because they are tart, not as sweet as strawberries, there is an inclination to add sugar. Using honey is much better for you; and the result may be better because of the cohesiveness of the honey.

Top to Bottom: Huckleberry, Coastal Huckleberry, Blueberry

Brambles (**Blackberries** and **Raspberries** etc.) (Rubus species): If you have not made a day outing of picking blackberries in late summer you have truly missed out on one of life's bittersweet moments. Our Northwest is a good place for berry hunters, especially on the west side of the Cascades, the Coast Range and nearly all of the way to the sea. You can find naturalized blackberries on the east side of the Cascade Slope; they are just not as prevalent. However, we found an abundance of them growing in Hell's Canyon. The berries were large and sweet.

We always pick way more than we need but the pies, jams, syrup and bags of frozen berries last us through to next summer. These purple morsels are sought after by many, from birds to bears. In fact, in places we have lived, we've had to be careful to let the bears have what they want first. There are numerous varieties of blackberry such as the Himalayan and blackcap varieties. Other wild berries are wild raspberry, thimbleberry, salmonberry.

These berries are a great source of Vitamin C, tannic acid, and fiber. Most require some caution in picking. My outfit usually includes shorts, short sleeved T-shirt and sandals. This isn't very smart, but it is usually very hot out. We often stop to pick berries on a whim, unprepared.

Most of these berries grow on very unforgiving thorny vines or brambles. The thorns seem to have a great desire to make it hard for you to extract the sweet fruit. I always discover that the best berries are just out of reach and protected by a fierce assembly of thorns. Proper clothing for serious picking would be long sleeved shirts and long pants, preferably out of a material less likely to snag. Gloves with the fingers cut out and even a hat is necessary because often the brambles grow taller than the average person. You ought to see my "blackberry jeans"; there isn't a spot that hasn't been snagged or stained.

It is also important to pick in areas that have not been sprayed with herbicides or that is away from the pollution of automobile exhaust. Large sheets of cardboard or plywood help to negotiate into the better spots where others haven't picked.

Parts used: berries, leaves, bark. Gather some young leaves for a great tea, either alone or added to other herbs. Try adding berry leaves to your favorite tea.

White to pinkish blossoms appear as early as April and berries come on starting midsummer. While you are out walking in the spring you can take note of the flowering vines with the idea in mind of where the best places will be for late summer picking. On plants that have received an abundance of winter and spring rains and plenty of summer sun, the berries will be larger and sweeter.

The bark is used for medicinal purposes by herbalists who extract the tannic acid for an elixir to treat a variety of lower intestinal complaints.

Best use for berries is just fresh, washed and cooled. Pies and such desserts are great. Try to avoid much use of sugar. In baking, try using honey.

My wife uses her old ice cream maker to make blackberry ice cream, and with some chopped local grown nuts thrown in, ambrosia!

Salmonberry in bloom

Blackberry (Thimbleberry variety) in bloom

Along the Path

Considering the thorn: "Other seed fell among the thorns which grew up and choked the plants." (Matthew 13:7) I can come out of a session of berry picking looking like I have been in battle—bloody and injured. This is another example of the fact that God's creation is there to remind us of much. While it would be easy to curse during those picking sessions, it is better to be reminded that we live under the curse because of sin. This is a curse that God will overturn someday.

It is also good to remember the suffering that our Lord endured, not just by nails and spear, but by sharp thorns as well. He did it willingly, on our behalf and because no greater love could be demonstrated. Jesus states these words about his willingness: "Greater love has no one than this, that he lay down his life for his friends. You are my friends." (John 15:13-14) I will pick berries again and I will get stuck and scratched again; but when that happens perhaps I will remember the stanza of the old hymn: "What a friend we have in Jesus."

Buffalo Berry, Silver (Shepherdia argentea), Canada or Russet Buffalo berry (S. canadensis) Round-leaf Buffalo berry (S. rotundifolia): Native to North America. Its habitat stretches from New England through the Great Plains, the Rockies and in the West from New Mexico to Washington, all parts of Canada and in Alaska. Evergreen shrub. Oval, shiny leaves and orange or red fruit, quite tart.

The silver buffalo berry is more palatable. A silvery, oval-leaved evergreen shrub with dull thorns and bright red fruit.

Russet buffalo berry is a thornless, dull-green evergreen with indistinct flowers that produce shiny berries. Extreme bitter taste, though it sweetens after frost. Named for the berries' use as a seasoning and tenderizer of buffalo meat.

Parts used: Berries, tart but tasty, eaten fresh or used for jams, jellies, sauces.

Bunchberry (Cornus canadensis) Western Bunchberry aka Dwarf Dogwood (C. unalaschkensis): Exotic greens and reds make up this small forest dweller, which reminds me of Christmas. The 4-blossom white flower, protruding from the center of a circle or whorl of broad leaves, is a spring wonder to behold. The plant grows less than a foot tall. In the East and the West grows in shady, moisture-rich forests and bogs.

Parts used: The whole plant. The berries, which grow in a single cluster, are edible though bland compared to the plant's striking looks. Good food value. The leaves and some of the top root are gathered and dried for tea. The plant's aspirin-like qualities act as an anti-inflammatory, yet it is easy on the digestive system. The berries can be mixed with other fruits in jams, jellies, and syrups. Topically, use as a poultice; the crushed berries are effective for burns, rashes, poison oak and other skin maladies.

Burdock, Common (Arctium minus) Great Burdock (A. lappa): Transplant from Europe. Biannual. The second year it sprouts pink or purple thistle-like flower heads. Grows everywhere; prefers drier settings. Will grow to 4 feet tall. Broad, pointed leaves.

Parts used: The whole plant. Foragers consider this a great food plant. The roots are cooked in soups, the leaves used in salads, and the stalks cooked like asparagus or sliced for a stir fry. Roots are gathered before the plant sends up its stalk; you need to know what it looks like or where you spotted it the year before. As a medicinal, burdock root is used as a whole-body tonic with emphasis on the stabilization of the liver, as a diuretic, for clearing the lungs, as a blood purifier, and is good for the skin. Some people infuse chopped burdock in apple cider vinegar to make a wonderful vinaigrette and marinade.

Butternut (Juglans cinerea) Black Walnut (J. nigra) California Black Walnut (J. hindsii) Arizona Walnut (J. rupestris major): These are deciduous trees, regal in their beauty and bountiful in their fruit, if you can get those stubborn shells open.

Butternut, a native, is part of the greater walnut family. Butternut, in the East can be found from Canada, south to Georgia, and west to Minnesota.

Black walnut is native to much of the East but has been transplanted and cultivated in most places in the U.S. California black walnut is found sporadically throughout Northern California. Arizona (or Nogal) walnut is indigenous to Arizona, New Mexico, Utah and Texas. The trees tend to be large and spreading, with furrowed bark. The long leaves are divided into serrated spear-shaped leaflets in groups of 9 to 19, depending on the variety. The nuts are round and furrowed-looking like the human brain.

Parts used: Bark, leaves and fruit. Black walnut bark infused as a tea helps to relieve constipation and bacterial and parasitic infections. It can also be used as a mouthwash for sores of the mouth and inflamed tonsils. An infusion of butternut bark acts as a soothing laxative. It may also help treat the symptoms from a cold. Nuts are good for fighting against high cholesterol. Used as an astringent, the leaves of the black walnut help to treat warts, eczema, herpes, psoriasis and ringworm. The healing potential for walnut may go even farther, as suggested by eminent herbalist Dr. James Duke. They may be a good diet aid and have even been used to treat thyroid problems.

Black Walnut

Butternut leaves

Cactus (Cactacae): Barrel (Ferocactus species), Cholla (Cylindroopuntia species) Hedgehog (Echinocereus species) Organ Pipe (Stenocereus thurberi) Prickly Pear (Opuntia species) Saguaro (Carnegiea gigantean): As Northerners we have come to love our visits to the desert Southwest in the winter. I am fascinated by the flora of the area. It is rich, diverse and surprisingly plentiful and beneficial to man and beast. Cactus can be quite a treat, but gathering edible and medicinal parts can be formidable.

Cactus, considered a Southwest desert plant, is found from Californian to New Mexico. Some cacti range farther. In my state of Oregon, hedgehog and prickly pear cactus are found in rarity, in some mild, high desert areas. We have discovered them in Hells Canyon and in and around John Day Fossil Beds National Monument.

There are numerous varieties of barrel cactus to be found. They are similar to an old keg style barrel but armed with hundreds of needle-sharp quills ready to defend their being. Nonetheless, natives and immigrants soon learned how to utilize them. Contrary to some old westerns I have seen, lopping off the top of a cactus to get to some water was rarely done.

The flowering fruit is an offering worth trying. At the top of the barrel cactus beautiful flowers bloom in oranges, reds and yellows, depending upon the variety. Once the fruit has formed from the flower they can be extracted carefully. The fruit can be consumed, though it is somewhat bitter. It can be pulverized and made into such things as a paste for candy. The seeds can be eaten. Native people would parch the seeds, and then grind them for use as flour.

Cholla is formidable looking and it is claimed by the many victims of its quills that the plant jumps out to grab you. It is also edible . . . sort of. The natives and adventurous immigrants pick the new buds. These have a lot fewer spines. They also have little hairs known as glochids that are like little slivers of wood that are hard to extract. All of this obviously needs to be removed before you even think about consuming them. The buds are roasted and then rolled on a hard surface to finish removing any glochids and spines left. The fruit can be eaten, but you must be careful in the handling to make sure nothing that will harm you is still there. I think I will just look at them from a safe distance.

Hedgehog cactus, which is one of the farthest-ranging cacti, is identifiable by its multiple stems. A smaller cactus, it grows from just a few inches tall to a few feet. When fully ripe the small fruit of this plant is prized by humans and wildlife. The fruit pretty much loses all of its spines, making it readily edible. It is also very sweet, which is not always the case with cacti.

The majestic organ pipe cactus, which grows in just the warmest areas of the Sonoran Desert, is characterized by its size and the many branches that shoot up from the main stalk. Its fruit is edible. Once ripe, the spines fall off by themselves. Most, if not all the area where organ pipe grows is protected, so it would be wise to only gather the fruit after checking applicable local codes and laws.

Prickly pear is one of the most sought after cacti for its edible parts. The fruit is wonderful but also the leaves known as "pads" are gathered. These edible parts are considered quite medicinal as well because of the high content of vitamin A and C found in the fruit and the mucilage in the pads. The mucilage may help control and regulate blood pressure and cholesterol levels.

The fruits, looking like little colorful pears, are covered in the notorious glochids or hairs that must be removed. The pads are covered not only with spines, but glochids as well.

The fruit is quite good, especially when pulverized and made into jellies or candy. The pads, which are eaten by those who have the know-how, have so far confounded me about the best way to make them palatable.

Saguaro, the giant beauty of the Sonoran is full of fruit that is highly desirable to humans and animals. When ripe, the fruit is shaped like miniature, spiny, red watermelons. The pulp is reminiscent of a fig and is very sweet and can be eaten raw or cooked for a number of uses.

Varieties of Cacti
Top: Saguaro, Barrel   Middle: Hedgehog, Prickly Pear
Bottom: Cholla with fruit, Bird's nest in Cholla.

Calamus (Acorus calamus) aka Sweet Flag: This is a wondrous plant made by a benevolent God. Calamus can be found most everywhere in and around ponds and wetlands. It is abundantly available. The benefits as a food and an herb are almost unequalled. The plant has yellowish, shiny leaves, which would remind you of iris. You may notice a spike or spadix growing from the side of it, at an angle, and looking a bit like the top of the cattail plant. The plant has a very pungent, spicy aroma. This is important to know so you can distinguish it from blue flag, which grows in similar habitat, but is poisonous.

Parts used: The stalk is cut and peeled into small portions then boiled for some time, with a few changes of water, to make it tender. This plant has been used for years and years to make a sweet confection by combining syrup and simmering together for 20 minutes to make sweet flag candy. The new shoots can be used in salads. The root is used for medicinal purposes for all kinds of digestive issues, from the top to the bottom of your tract. Use a tablespoon of the root steeped in hot water and drink as a tea.

Cattail, common (Typha latifolia): Cattails exist nearly everywhere there is abundant water supply to support them, such as ponds, wetlands and irrigations ditches. Cattail is easily spotted and usually grows in great colonies. Look for the brown stalk, which is actually the flower head of many minute flowers. The cattail shoots can grow tall, over the average person's head.

Parts used: Much of the plant is edible. Many naturalists and wildcrafters consider cattail THE best wild plant for food. In spring the young shoots are used by peeling them down to the white core. The flower spikes, or what will eventually become the brown "cat tails," can be boiled like you would corn on the cob and eaten the same way. The pollen can be gathered by shaking it into a container.

Foragers gather the rootstalks from late fall to early spring. They wash them, peel off the outer layer, then crush the core in water removing the fibers from the starch. This process is repeated until you end up with a clean, white, starchy substance that is the consistency of flour, which can be used for baking in a manner similar to other flours.

Celery, wild (Apium graveolens) aka Smallage: The debate is still on: Is wild celery naturalized or native? Either way, if you find real celery in the wild, then good for you! Wild celery resembles what you might buy in the store, only it's wilder and freer looking, especially as it blooms and goes to seed. The flower heads are large umbels of small white petals. You should notice the distinct, strong aroma of celery or parsley—steer clear if you don't. There are a number of poisonous plants with similar looks.

Parts used: The whole plant for culinary and medicinal purposes. I believe that celery is one of the best vegetable herbs you can consume, truly one of God's super foods. The raw stalks are not very edible unless you find new, young ones. They can be cooked. Medicinally, the fluid can be expressed from them and utilized for a number of purposes. The leaves are great for culinary dishes. The seeds are used for both culinary and medicinal purposes. Celery seed is a good alternative to the salt shaker. It is said to help with bronchitis and has been used in days past for treatment of cold, flu, water retention, arthritis, spleen and liver. Celery acts as a diuretic and a pain killer. It has a cleansing effect upon the whole body, helps with weight regulation, and improves the skin.

Warning: Some people are allergic to celery. Wild celery is strong; a little goes a long way.

Note: For purposes of clarification, I will mention here that there are a number of wild plants that are often popularly called "wild celery" that are not celery at all. I often hear "wild celery" mentioned, when what is actually being talked about is cow-parsnip or celery-leafed lovage. Another plant called "wild celery" is Vallisneria americana, American eelgrass, which is an aquatic plant that is not edible. This plant looks more like a grass with long flat slender leaves. It grows mostly under water. It is an important food source for wildlife. If you are on the East Coast and catch a bass in some area like the Chesapeake Bay you will likely pull up some of this plant in the process.

American Eelgrass is *not* edible

Along the Path

More than likely celery was originally used as one of the bitter herbs in the Passover feast. Perhaps the Israelites didn't know just how good of an herbal it was for them. Sometimes God puts us through bitter times that are actually for our betterment. We have to remember that this is a fallen world, cursed by sin. Bad things happen all the time. As you know and I know, none of us is immune.

These events can make us bitter towards God and others; or we can allow God to make the bitter things of life a blessing to us. Perhaps we don't see it or understand, but we can trust that God uses bad things to make good things for us. How else would we know the difference?

As God's children we are to get rid of such things as bitterness that our hearts may harbor. There is good reason for this. We are to replace such negatives with compassion and forgiveness. This is the constant reminder of what Christ did for us when we least deserved it. Proverbs 14:10 states, "Each heart knows its own bitterness."

We all deal with something. It may be personal pain or loss. It could be a disappointment so big that the memory of it doesn't fade. It could be anger or woe over a situation, a person, one's own self, or perhaps God himself. Bitterness will hold us down, stop us in our tracks, and choke the very life out of us if we harbor it. Instead we need to get rid of it and replace it with the joy that God provides for us in all situations. So that's what we do: we get up, get going and holding on to this promise. "For the Lord your God will bless you in all your harvest and in all the work of your hands, and your joy will be complete." (Deuteronomy 16:15) The antidote to bitterness is allowing God to provide joy. And he will.

Chamomile (Asteraceae species): A favorite herb for my garden and for my health and well being. Chamomile tea is one of life's great pleasures. The aroma of the flower and foliage is an almost-citrus to sweet-apple smell. Also known as pineapple weed and ground apple. There are three most common varieties of this plant: wild chamomile, a small plant that hugs the ground and is the one you find the most in  the wild; German chamomile (Chamaemelum nobile), the tall cousin, found many places in the wild too, an assumed escapee from the garden; Roman chamomile, an in-between size, also of the Chamaemelum nobile family.

All three have the distinct, sweet scent of flower and leaf. The flower looks like a small, delicate daisy—white petals with a yellow center and feathery leaves. It is believed that wild chamomile (Matricaria discoidea) is native to the West. This plant prefers moist meadow areas but is quite hardy and adapts to diverse conditions. A true flower of summer, when the most and the best are found. We find it in abundance on the eastern side of the Cascades in the high desert regions. Many daisy-type flowers are out there. If you find something that looks similar, but doesn't have the sweet scent, it's probably not chamomile.

Chamomile is a calmative, digestive aid, and sleep aid. Although sweet, it's a pretty powerful herb that helps cure a disturbed digestive system.

If you have some leftover chamomile tea, rinse your hair with it. It's as good for the hair as for the stomach. The dried flowers make a great aromatic addition to potpourri. If you end up with a scrape or a bug bite you might try rubbing the flower directly on the injured area. Absolute best use for the plant, and specifically the flowers, is as a sweet, golden tea.

Gather some, but not all, flowers from the plants. Use the flowers fresh or dried, infused with hot water, and steeped for refreshing hot or cold tea. As you are gathering you may find sweet meadow mints as well. This combination makes for one of the finest teas you could drink, refreshing, uplifting, and healthy for the digestive system, top to bottom.

Cheeseweed, Buttonweed, Little Mallow, (Malva neglecta) Bull Mallow (M. borealis): Part of the mallow family, this plant gets its name from the fruit which looks like small cheese wheels. This non-native, invasive plant grows pretty much everywhere. You probably won't need to go out in the wild to find it—no

further than your own yard. The stems grow prostrate to the ground. The rounded lobed leaves give the appearance of a geranium or hibiscus. I had one sprout up uninvited in a plant pot. The flowers are octagonal, bluish white, looking like a miniature mallow flower that you might cultivate in your herb garden.

Parts used: Leaves and stems are cooked; similar in taste and texture to okra. They are also used as a topical skin soother.

Tea can be made from the leaves and stems and is found to be quite pleasant and refreshing. You will find it a bit slimy; but like slippery elm tea, it is soothing to a raw throat. The tea also acts as a stomach tonic. The little fruits can be eaten when new and still green.

Wild Fire Pin Cherry
(bright red when ripe)

Cherry, Wild (Prunus species) Chokecherry (P. Virginiana) Black Cherry (P. serotina) Pin or Fire Cherry (P. pensylvanica) Bitter Cherry (P. emarginata): This genus is one of the most widely distributed fruit trees in the U.S. Chokecherries can be found most everywhere along river banks and moist areas of forests. They often grow as a small tree or a shrub, 2 to 12 feet tall, in thickets. In the springtime, the bushes are easy to find because of the wonderful blossoms and the aroma they exude. The flowers grow in long clusters of white; and the color of the fruit can be dark red, to purple, to even ebony. The leaves are small, a few inches in length and oblong.

Bitter cherry, which truly lives up to its name, grows in much of the West, on both the east and west side of the Cascades. The ones that grow east of the Cascades are shrubs. We have found them in many places in the Lava Beds National Monument in far Northern California. The leaves are smaller than chokecherry and somewhat oval, but wider at the end and usually curled. Spring flowers are found in flat clusters of white to pink petals. The fruit is small, ½ inch or less in diameter and usually bright red.

Wild cherries have a high carbohydrate value and high antioxidant levels.

Parts used: You can eat the fruit, fresh from the bush, if you can stand the pucker. It is much better in jams, jellies and sauces. The bark has been used as a tea to treat respiratory complaints. The inner bark is steeped in hot but not boiling water. Warning: the seeds and wilted leaves evidently contain cyanide.

Bitter Cherry

Black Chokecherry

Red Chokecherry

Chickweed, Common (Stellaria media): Very likely you won't have to travel far to find this incredible, beneficial plant—maybe no farther than your front yard. Look in damp, partially shaded areas. This familiar lawn weed nuisance is an amazing little plant, and not just in its ability to spread all over the place.

Not native to the U.S., but has been naturalized. This is a low, spreading plant that may grow to a little more than a foot in height. The plant has small oval leaves and little white star-shaped flowers. It is hardy and will grow most of the year round. In the harsher climates you find chickweed as the first plant that sprouts. It grows just about everywhere.

It was once used as feed for fowl, especially during the winter months. Another name for the plant is "winterweed" because it really begins its largest growth spurt during the fall, through winter and then, bang, come spring and the stuff is all over the place. Most people consider it a garden nuisance. If they would take some time to sample it, they might change their minds. Early spring is the best time to gather it. When you are wishing for some fresh, home-grown greens, then chickweed can fill the bill.

Parts used: The new leaves, picked before flowers form, for salads or cooked greens. Full of mineral salts plus Vitamin C, iron, calcium, potassium, etc. Considered a medicinal herb for its anti-inflammatory potential for treating diseases such as arthritis and rheumatism. It may be an effective tonic for the kidneys and for proper liver function. Externally, applied as an ointment or poultice, it is good for skin irritations.

The use of chickweed is enjoying a new popularity. I have seen a number of imaginative recipes that call for its use—from simple salad, to pesto, to quiche. Try the recipe below if you are wishing it was pesto season, but it's too early to grow basil.

Sarah Campbell's Chickweed Pesto

2 to 4 cups fresh, clean chickweed
$\frac{1}{2}$ to 1 cup walnuts
$\frac{1}{4}$ to $\frac{1}{2}$ cup grated Parmesan cheese
2 to 4 cloves of garlic to taste
$\frac{1}{2}$ cup extra virgin olive oil
1 teaspoon powdered kelp
$\frac{1}{2}$ teaspoon ground black pepper

Place all ingredients in a food processor or blender and blend until smooth.

Along the Path

Chickweed is a common plant and often a bane to gardeners and people fastidious about their lawns. Isn't it true, though, that some things don't always seem to be what they really are. Chickweed is of great value and yet it is not seen that way. If you are a believer in Jesus then you also know that there is an expectation that you will somehow be a witness for him and the Kingdom of Heaven. Many of us feel we have little to offer. That is the point, though. Through his enabling, by the work of the Holy Spirit, God makes us worthy vessels for his service and praise. Scripture teaches us that we can come as we are, just being simple and humble enough to say, "Okay, Lord, I am not sure what I have to offer you, but here I am." 1 Corinthians 1:27 is a great lesson, especially if you are feeling down and useless: "But God chooses the foolish things of the world to shame the wise."

My first thought on this was, "If all God wants is a fool like me, then here I am." You see, it is not what you have; it is what God will do with what you have. I have heard remarkable stories about how humble, simple people have witnessed in such ways as to sway the powerful, beautiful and wealthy into getting their relationship with God in right order. Like chickweed—common as can be and considered a nuisance, yet it has incredible abilities. With God, our abilities, talents and gifts can do incredible things.

Chicory (Cichorium intybus): This could easily have been one of the bitter herbs described in the book of Exodus, to be used in the Passover meal that Jehovah God instituted. This plant looks similar to bachelor's button but it is not. Chicory may have a number of small daisy-shaped, pale blue to violet flowers on one stem while bachelor's button usually has one flower per stem. This plant has naturalized and grows everywhere, especially dry, sunny areas. It is definitely drought tolerant and doesn't mind poor soil. You can find it taking up vacant fields or along roadsides. It is considered a nuisance by some because it has been very invasive since introduced to North America. If you had lived a few generations back, you probably would have been much more informed about it. The dried roots, gathered in the spring, were used as a coffee substitute when coffee was hard to come by or just too expensive.

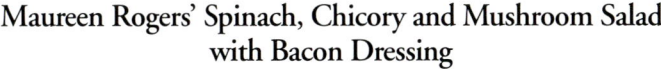

Parts used: Young leaves, gathered in the spring, for salads or cooked like other greens. Chicory is also a cultivated garden plant, used as a salad green.

The leaves and flowers can be used for a poultice for external inflammations of the skin. The root of the plant is split and dried, roasted and then pulverized and used as a tea. This is perhaps its best use. It is mildly diuretic and also considered a liver tonic. If coffee is doing a job on your stomach, try a chicory-based tea. You may find that it is not only easier on you but that it might help to settle and heal stomach and digestive issues.

Chicory is roasted for 30 minutes at 250°, and then ground. My grandmother lived well into her nineties and drank this every day.

Maureen Rogers' Spinach, Chicory and Mushroom Salad with Bacon Dressing

2 cups baby spinach and chicory leaves per person
2 strips of bacon per person
Fresh mushrooms, the amount as desired
Olive Oil
Red Wine Vinegar
Sea Salt and freshly ground Pepper

Wash and thoroughly drain spinach and chicory. Fry bacon until crisp. Reserve about 3 tablespoons of the bacon fat to add to the dressing. Slice the mushrooms. Make a dressing with the oil, vinegar, bacon fat, salt and pepper. Toss with the greens and the mushrooms and crumble the bacon over it.

Along the Path

I have grown chicory in my garden for the root and the leaves. However, I find the leaves are pretty bitter and a little too strong for my salad taste buds. As mentioned above, it may very well have been used in the original Passover meal and most certainly for Passover meals over the millenniums. If it was used originally, it would certainly have made a point. The purpose of the bitter herbs was a reminder to the captive nation of Israel about the bitterness of slavery. If you recall from the Exodus story, as the people started their journey to the Promised Land, they began to grumble. When the journey became difficult, they complained and missed what they had in Egypt, forgetting the bitterness of slavery. For we who are believers in Christ, and we who know he needed to die for our sin, this bitter herb is a good reminder of the enslavement of sin and its negative effect upon our lives.

Sometimes, when the journey gets tough, it is easy to slip back into thinking about the sinful things you may have done and desire them again. If you slip, and most of us do at least once, we are quickly reminded of the bitterness of sin and the absence of God's presence in that sin. In these cases bitter is better. This bitter taste reminds us of what we lose if we have turned back to our old ways which we might somehow remember as sweet. It might seem strange, but say this with me: "Bitter is better, bitter is better."

Chiltepin (Capsicum annuum glabriusculum): This plant is the wild ancestor of the fiery peppers many of us love to use to spice up our foods. Chiltepin is a rare plant in the U.S. and only found in a few places. This capsicum is considered by some to be the mother of all peppers. You can find the plant growing in Arizona, New Mexico and Texas. If you get over the border to Sonora, Mexico, you can find them in much more abundance. We spotted some of these plants in the Buenos Aires National Wildlife Refuge near Aravaca Arizona in the far southern portion of the state.

The plant grows to 6 feet in height, preferring areas that offer shade and moisture. The leaves resemble a typical pepper plant leaf. The plant blossoms small white flowers that develop into a pea-like fruit. These little peas are the peppers.

If gathered and consumed early, the peppers won't take your head off. As they mature, their fire increases incredibly. The Scoville heat unit on these is higher than the habañero but not as hot as the infamous ghost pepper. They provide food for birds and wildlife that don't seem to be affected by the capsicum as we are.

Parts used: The fruit, for food, used as you would use cultivated peppers. Medicinally (and surprisingly), hot peppers are good for aiding digestion and boosting metabolism.

Clover, Red (Trifolium pretense) and White (Trifolium repens) and about 300 other varieties: In these days when cancer affects so many of us, this abundant plant is a serious cancer fighter. It has been used as a food and for beverages for millenniums. Clover is one of the most abundant of plants, growing naturally and cultivated worldwide. It has been used more for animal fodder. I am convinced that humans ought to be using it specifically in the fight against the worldwide plague of cancer. You can find one species or another, nearly everyplace in North America. Some species are native; others are naturalized.

Red Clover

White Clover

Most clover looks as you expect: bulbous, compact flower heads and three leaflets reminiscent of a shamrock. The plant grows in heights from a few inches to 2 feet tall. The flowers are often one of the first to bloom in the spring and may last well into fall, depending upon the climate. I grow red clover in my backyard because the grass seed I have tried on numerous occasions just doesn't do well. The red clover has. I have noticed now that the common white clover has infiltrated from somewhere.

Parts used: Flowers. As kids, my friends and I would suck on the sweet flowers. My bees love them. If you have ever tasted clover honey, then you know there is nothing much better. Just simply to take the flower and chew it, is another story. It's hard to chew, and not particularly digestible. However, you can take the fresh flower petals and leaves and shred them and add them to a salad. You may think you are grazing the lawn, but the health benefits are worth it. You can soak the leaves or gently boil a few minutes in salty water to make them more palatable. The dried flowers make a great tea. People have taken those same flower heads and seeds and have ground them for a very nutritious flour.

As a medicinal, clover shines. It is such a powerful antioxidant and cancer fighter that it can actually stop tumors from growing and even cause them to shrink. This happens because of the high content of Genistein which is an Isoflavone that has been studied and noted for its help in fighting cancer. Clover has also been used to help break the tobacco habit. Amazing to think what a little clover tea might do for you.

Sweet Clover, White (Melilotus alba), Yellow (M. officianlis): These clovers are not related to red and white clover and do not look like them, either. Both are tall plants growing to heights of 5 to 8 feet. The leaves are oblong and oval. The many small flowers grow on the long stems and are either white or yellow in color. These naturalized plants grow pretty much everywhere.

Bees keep busy all summer in fields and vacant lots full of these pretty, vanilla-scented plants, producing from the nectar a light, mild honey. Sweet clover, besides being a major honey plant, is used by farmers as a cover crop and for animal forage. They are found as escapees in many places.

Parts used: Before the flower develops, the leaves are good fresh in salads or lightly cooked as a green. They can be dried and used as a sweet spice. After the long season of bloom, the seeds can be gathered and used as a seasoning. As a medicinal sweet clover is a digestive aid, an expectorant for congestion, and a diuretic. It is also used topically as a poultice or salve for a variety of skin problems and injuries.

Coltsfoot, Common (Tussilago farfara, Petasites palmatus), Western or Sweet (P. speciosa): Have a cough? Then cover your mouth; and have some coltsfoot. In the East look for large, palm-shaped leaves; in the West look for divided leaves like that of the maple. Both leaves are bright green above, a satiny silver color below. Distinctive yellow flowers are ringed with many minute petals. In the West (Tussilago farfara variety), the flower is purplish to white. The small, bell-shaped flower head has numerous petals. The flower looks a bit like a dandelion but is much more dainty, with petals like fine hairs. This plant loves the moist wet woods and bogs where it usually grows in colonies. In the West it grows on the west side of the mountains from Northern California north into Canada.

If you are out looking in the early spring, close to the ground, then you might see the purple-tinged, unfurled flower stems rising first, then the leaves come next, seeming to erupt directly from the ground.

Parts used: Cook the edible leaf stalks and flower stems as you would asparagus. For medicinal use, chop and steep the leaves and stalks as a very effective treatment for coughs, sore throats, and the stuffiness associated with a cold.

Caution: The coltsfoot, comfrey concern: Both of these plants have come under fire in the last couple of decades because they contain P.A. or the Pyrrolizidine alkaloids chemicals at higher levels than other plants. P.A.s are considered toxic and carcinogenic. But as noted

herbalist James Duke indicates, you would find more P.A.s in a glass of beer. I suspect the amount of beer consumed by Americans is way, way higher than that of coltsfoot. Just another reminder that we live in a fallen world affected by sin; life and all that is in it—even the good things—can hold a degree of danger. We need water daily; yet, this same life-giving substance can drown you.

Columbine (Aquilegia vulgaris, formosa): Columbine seems to be an herb that is of minimal usefulness to us. Maybe we just have not discovered enough about it. I include it, though, because it is my favorite wildflower. It is a beauty to discover in the wild. Perhaps all you will do is just admire it and take a photo. This flower can be found in most of the West, from sub-alpine heights to the high desert and down to the sea. Columbine prefers a shady to semi-shady place where water is plentiful. This is a true wildflower in appearance and hardiness. Blue columbine is the state flower of Colorado. There are numerous varieties of this flower, showing off in colors of yellow, pink, blue, purple and red.

Columbine tends to be low growing, but with the right conditions can reach heights of 3 feet. What is so striking about the plant are the leaves and flowers. It has a branched multi-fibrous root. The stems are unique, dark green to blackish color and rather stout. From there is a large mass of leaves, also dark and of a bluish green on the top and grey underneath. These lowest leaves are on long foot-stalks and are large having a terminal group of three. The leaflets might remind you of an exotic clover leaf. The plant blossoms in early spring, usually one of the first found if you grow them in your garden. The flowers will last until mid to late summer. Once the bloom is gone, the pea pod-like fruit contains numerous seeds which will produce abundantly in the right conditions. The scientific name of Aquilegia comes from a word that has to do with an eagle, specifically in reference to the flowers which resemble a talon. Hummingbirds and butterflies favor this plant greatly. In the garden it may be the clarion call to these creatures to come for a visit.

Parts used: Flowers, stems and roots. Tea from the root is said to help with diarrhea. As a topical it is used in salve form for rheumatism and the edible flowers can grace a salad or desert.

Comfrey (Symphytum officinale): This big showy plant grows about everywhere, preferring meadows and damp areas. Those who have grown herbs for some time usually have comfrey in their herb gardens. In times past it was a widely used herb. These days it has fallen in popularity. (See the warning below.) This plant can grow to 4 feet in the best conditions, and spreads in many places. The tongue-shaped dull green leaves protrude from the center, looking like a big mound of green tongues. The flowers form under the leaves and are white to lavender and shaped like tubes.

Parts used: The leaves and the sap from the rootstalk. The young leaves can be eaten like spinach. The leaves can be made into a tea and also used topically to treat a variety of skin issues.

Warning: There has been much concern that comfrey can contribute to the development of liver cancer. Some countries have banned the use and sale of the plant altogether.

Cottonwood or Poplar, also see Aspen (Populus): There are a number of varieties of this tree throughout the U.S. and Canada. Most leaves are heart shaped or oval, with distinct veins. The flower is where the name comes from, because they shed this fluff all over the place. Cottonwood and poplar grow best in areas where sufficient water is available. They may line a stream or lake or take up a meadow or field.

Parts used: Leaf buds and the inner bark. As an edible, the inner bark and sap. As a medicinal, cottonwood contains salicylates. Great as an anti-inflammatory, both internal and topical (for sprains, muscle stress, etc.). Used to treat respiratory complaints.

Cow Parsnip (Heracleum maximum) aka Indian celery: This plant is easy to identify if you know your wild carrot or Queen Anne's lace. The flower looks similar, but the plant can reach herculean proportions. The huge umbel flowers have a strong, perhaps disagreeable aroma or odor, depending on how your olfactory senses interpret it. The flowers are perched on huge, thick stems. Cow parsnip's white flower can grow to 8 inches wide, made up of small clusters of petals. The leaves, shaped somewhat like maple leaves, are tinged with purple. In the best conditions, the stalks can grow to 10 feet. Cow parsnip grows across the U.S. in moist areas.

Parts used: The whole plant. Cook stems and leaves as you would celery. Cook roots, like carrots, in a few changes of water. Even the seeds are edible, crushed as a seasoning. Medicinally, the seeds are used to treat mouth sores and inflammations.

Warning: Looks like water hemlock, which is very poisonous. It can be found growing in the same habitat, but water hemlock has a musty odor. And, while cow parsnip grows a single root like a carrot, hemlock tends to grow in bunches, and the crushed flowers smell like something that has been overrun by mice: pretty disgusting.

Crabapple (Malus species): I've observed crabapple trees being used more often as yard ornamentals. Today the use of crabapple fruit is minimal, much less than in days gone by. We are missing out on a viable and abundant food source with healing qualities. Crabapples are part of the greater rose family, related to hawthorn, and cousins or parents of our domestic apple.

There are perhaps as many as fifty varieties and many of them native to the U.S. They are found in nearly every state in the U.S. Crabapple trees tend to be smaller than our cultivated varieties; some are not much more than shrubs. The leaves tend to be more oblong and usually toothed. Easiest way to notice them in the wild is in spring when the bloom is on and the trees are filled with an abundance of five-petal, pink or white flowers. These flowers provide much nectar and honey; Mason bees are usually found in abundance. This

is necessary or there would be no fruit. The fruit are small, round or oblong, and red, green or yellow.

Parts used: The sour fruit is hard to eat fresh. But it contains high levels of pectin, good for use in jams, jellies and syrups, alone or combined with sweeter fruits. Or make old-fashioned pickled or spiced crabapples.

Cranberry, Bog (Vaccinium oyxcoccos), Mountain Cranberry (V. vitis-idaea), High Bush Cranberry (Viburnum trilobum): Cranberry is another of God's super fruits with goodness packed inside! You can find them in the wild, near water or in mountains. While Americans have been eating them for centuries, resurgence of popularity has come with greater knowledge of the benefits. Closely related to blueberry, bilberry and huckleberry.

Bog cranberry is a low-lying shrub with vine-like branches. Leaves are oval but small. The plant produces indistinct, pinkish flowers. The fruit is small and deep red to pink. You are most likely to find these in sphagnum bogs of coastal mountains or seasides.

What is called high bush cranberry is not cranberry at all; it is part of the family of fruit that includes nannyberry and hobblebush. High bush is distinguished by the leaf's tri-fold shape, the bark's reddish smoothness, and the flower's 5 flat petals. The fruit looks and tastes like cranberry, red in appearance and tart in taste, though not nearly as tart as true cranberry. They can be eaten fresh and are often preferred to cranberries. They can

be made into jams or squeezed for juices. These plants have found their way into gardens and make for nice companions to blueberry plants. It is found as a native more in northern, moist mountain areas.

Parts used: The fruit of both are high in Vitamin C. Great medicinals for kidney and urinary tract issues. The bark is used for women's health and child bearing.

Creosote (Larrea divariata) or Chaparral: A common site in the desert Southwest at below 4,000 ft. In some areas, the only plant seen. In well-drained areas, the bushes can grow quite tall and in groves. Evergreen, with greasy to waxy yellow green leaves with a pungent aroma very noticeable after rain. When in bloom, the yellow flowers are about an inch wide with yellow petals. Often one of the first plants to bloom, starting in February. They in turn produce a small fruit which is round and fuzzy.

This hardy looking plant has been a blessing to the natives for centuries. European settlers have discovered many good qualities in this tough desert shrub. In optimum conditions it grows from just a few feet tall to perhaps 20 feet high. This plant may rule the day in its ability to be drought tolerant. It also lives a very long time, perhaps into thousands of years, competing with such ancients as bristlecone pine and giant sequoia. It has been a source of food, tools, and other things for Native Americans.

Parts used: Pretty much the whole plant. Leaves, stems and branches are infused into a tea that has been used to treat many complaints, if you can convince your mouth that the taste is okay to swallow. This same substance can be used topically to treat a number of skin issues and injuries.

Curly Dock or **Yellow Dock** (Rumex crispus): This is a familiar roadside weed that grows in most areas, preferring rich and moist soils. Related to rhubarb and sorrel. In some places, considered a nuisance. Not native, but naturalized to North America and Canada. Dock gets one of its names from its long, thick, yellow root. The plant grows to 3 feet with oblong pale-green leaves that have curly or wavy edges and bushy brown to green flowers on a long stalk.

Parts used: The raw leaves with their tart taste are used by hikers to extinguish thirst. They are better, though, cooked with mixed greens or, if you get to them early in the season, added to salads.

Medicinally the leaves are used as a topical for skin complaints such as itching and sores. The root is used as an astringent and has been helpful in the treatment of digestive issues and as a liver tonic. It is dried and pulverized and used as a tea.

A strong herb! A little goes a long way because of concern regarding oxalates that could cause poisoning. This is not a plant I would probably use much, other than the leaves topically or as a small addition to greens and salads.

Currant or **Gooseberry** (Ribes species): Perhaps it was our wet spring, but I do not remember a spring with more currant bushes. By mid-summer the female plants were loaded with pale red berries. The male plants just remain a thorny bunch ready to snag your pants or draw a little blood on some exposed skin. There are a number of varieties of this plant. Our east-of-the-Cascades variety is wax currant or squaw currant (Ribes cereum) and is predominantly, but not exclusively, a high desert or alpine bush. Distinguished by pale red berries on plants usually growing no more than 4 feet tall.

Ribes bracteosum or stink currant, which has bluish black fruit, tends to grow west of the Cascades. Ribes divaricatum is the coastal variety. Finally, there is Ribes viscosissimum which grows in much of the West except around Oregon's northern coast and coastal mountains and Washington's northern coast and coastal mountains. All varieties are considered natives of the area. The distinctive leaves look like small maple tree leaves which turn a pretty red in the fall. The flavor of the berries can range from quite sweet to very tart.

Parts used: Best uses are the berries cooked or dried for jams, jellies and such. As with most berries, fiber content is high, so they help the digestive system function well. I am told that currant tea helps relieve symptoms of the common cold. To make jams, cook the berries to make the seeds inside more palatable, or strain out the seeds. As with all berries, the less sugar you can use the better the medicinal properties; however, you will probably want to sweeten currants with the sweetener of your choice.

Top: Red Currant Bush
Middle: Red Currant Fruit
Bottom: Gooseberries

Dandelion (Taraxacum officinate): Nothing is more familiar than a dandelion with its spear-like leaves and yellow flower head, whose appearance like a lion's mane gives the plant its name. Not native to America, it arrived from Europe, where dandelion is cultivated as a crop. This plant grows everywhere in the U.S. Many people know it is edible, but have not tried it. Bitter tasting, it could have been one of the bitter herbs utilized in biblical-times Passover feasts. There are some real advantages to utilizing this herb, especially if you find it in the wild away from the pollutants, herbicides, and pesticides often present along city streets and yards.

Parts used: With their salty taste, the fresh young leaves gathered before the flower appears and added to a salad will help you keep from the salt shaker—if you need to cut down on salt. The flowers can be sautéed and eaten.

Dandelion acts as a diuretic and so helps with kidney and urinary function as well as conditions of high blood pressure. High in minerals and vitamins such as iron, potassium, calcium and other trace minerals. A good source of vitamin A. The plant contains lecithin, which helps with proper liver and gall bladder function. Cook the leaves like spinach. Try mixing with spinach, chard, collards, curly kale. As kids we would suck the nectar out of the stems. In the fall the plants can be dug and the roots harvested. You can either steep the roots in nearly boiling water or slowly bake them in an oven until they are toasty brown and brittle. These are ground and used for teas and for a coffee substitute.

LaDonna Lehman's Dandelion Jelly

4 cups fresh dandelion blossoms
2 tablespoons lemon juice
$5\frac{1}{2}$ cups Florida Crystals (unbleached vegan sugar)
$1\frac{3}{4}$ oz powdered pectin

In a stainless steel saucepan, boil the blossoms in 2 quarts water 4 to 5 minutes. Cool and strain, using care when pressing the liquid out of the flowers. Measure 3 cups of the liquid and place into a kettle. Add lemon juice and pectin. Bring mixture to a boil. Add the Florida Crystals and stir until dissolved. Bring to a rapid boil, stirring constantly. Reduce heat until mixture boils gently and stir 2½ minutes more. Remove from heat; pour jelly into prepared jelly glasses. Seal with paraffin; or cap with canning lids, then water-bath until sealed.

Daylily (Hemerocallis fulva): I love to grow daylilies in my gardens and I have an ever increasing number of them. Not only are they beautiful and hardy; they are a fine food source. In the wild they are a great find. The whole plant is edible. This is not considered a native plant, but has been in North America for hundreds of years and has naturalized in many places. In fact, in some places it is considered a toxic weed. It is named daylily because each bloom lasts but a day, opening as the sun rises and withering as the sun sets. Some day lilies are night bloomers. Daylily has a great, wild appearance; the tall leaves look more like young grass in the spring. In some milder places the plant grows and blossoms year round. The stem bears 3-petal flowers with same-color sepals (together called 'tepals'), in a variety of colors and shapes.

Parts used: Pretty much the whole plant. Daylilies have root tubers and early in the season these can be cooked and eaten like any starchy, steamed vegetable. The new shoots can be steamed like asparagus. The flower buds and the developed flowers can be cooked or eaten raw.

Along the Path

More than likely you have said or sang this verse before: "This is the day that the Lord has made." So, consider this: Jesus is our "Dayspring." What is a dayspring, you might ask? It is an old word for dawn that defines the sunrise. Dayspring has a greater symbolism; it was used as a description of the birth of Jesus. If he was born on or around Dec. 21, the shortest day of the year, then his birth also heralded the return of the sun as the days began to lengthen. It was the dawn of a new age. The birth of Christ and the formation of the Christian church did away with the Age of the Law and ushered in the Age of Grace.

So what do you see if you happen to be up for sunrise? I don't miss many of them. Do you just see the sun, our nearest star, rising over the horizon? Or do you see the evidence of a wonderful and benevolent Creator giving his people another day on planet earth to worship, serve, and make a God-positive difference for someone else?

In a section of Luke 12, Jesus instructs and encourages us. In verse 27 he says, "Consider how the lilies grow. They do not labor or spin. Yet I tell you not even Solomon in all his splendor was dressed like one of these." I like to think of this chapter as the "Don't worry, be happy" section of the Bible. In many ways our lives are like the daylily, short but yet they can be brilliant. We spend a lot of time worrying and fretting about many things that dull our luminance. If we only have this day, shouldn't we make it shine for Jesus who gives grace, forgiveness, and every resource and reason to "have a good day"?

Elderberry (Sambucus species): This hardy, under-story tree glows with brilliant white flowers spring and early summer. It then provides plentiful bunches of small berries in brilliant colors of red, blue, to nearly purple in late summer and fall—a sight to behold. Pinnate leaves with leaflets from 5 to 11 in number. The mature berries might remind you of a bunch of miniature grapes. Cut off bunches for easy picking. Many varieties: American elder, black elder, blue elder, red elder, dwarf elder, etc.

Most likely some species of elder grows in your area. It appreciates some shade and grows well beneath conifers and where water is readily available. We have seen them at sub-alpine heights, around great bodies of water like the Upper Klamath Lake and along the Snake River in Hells Canyon. Cooking improves the flavor of the berries. The seeds are considered toxic. Some use the fruit for elderberry wine; best used for juice, jams, jellies, and syrups. This retains the Vitamin A, B and C.

Parts used: Root, buds, leaves, flowers and berries. Elder has been considered the medicine chest of the country folks who used it medicinally, both internally and topically. Internally it is used as a blood tonic, digestive aid and for sufferers of constipation because it is a purgative. Topically the leaves have been used to treat cuts, scrapes, and other wounds. Some believe strongly that it hastens healing.

Caution is needed when using the root, leaves, and flowers internally, a little goes a long way. Too much upsets the stomach. But it has been used to treat colds, flu, and even tonsillitis. Research is continuing for its use in HIV treatment.

False Solomon's Seal (Smilacina racemosa): This beautiful plant comes with a warning. Not so much about this plant, but about the two poisonous plants that look very similar: Star of Bethlehem and fly-poison. The flowers of false Solomon's seal are the distinction you need to note. False Solomon's seal is a native plant found on both sides of the Rockies. The plant grows from rhizomes producing single branchless stems with grooved, oblong-shaped leaves with a distinct point. The white flowers have 6 petals. The fruit or berry matures from an unripe green to a deep red. This is a plant you will find in shady spots and along waterways. See also Solomon's seal.

Parts used: The young stems are stripped of leaves and lightly cooked as you would cook asparagus. The flavor might remind you of asparagus. The leaves are a digestive aid; but too many, and it acts as a laxative. The roots and berries are used also, but I would not recommend it. This is a beautiful plant. If found in abundance, and you want to try the stems, that could be fun; but it might be better just to admire and not pick. I tend to err on the side of caution. Other herbalists may tell you differently.

Fern, Fiddlehead or Ostrich (Matteucia struthiopteris): All kinds of ferns grow in most places of the U.S. Some are natives and many have come from abroad. The fern family is huge and varied. Frankly, I never thought about eating a fern and wondered about their medicinal benefits, if any. Where we live in the high desert area of Southern Oregon, ferns are few and far between; but there is a most unusual place to find some. We love going to the Lava Beds National Monument in the eastern part of far Northern California. This is an arid place punctured with many lava tube caves. In one of these caves coastal ferns grow in abundance—hundreds of miles from the nearest coast.

One fern that is popular and edible is the fiddlehead, also known as the ostrich fern. There are a number of ferns that sprout "fiddleheads." The unopened frond or the fawnis shaped like the scrolled top of a violin.

Fiddleheads can be taken from the ostrich fern as well as the bracken fern (Pteridium aquilinum), cinnamon or buckhorn fern which shoots up flowers that look like cinnamon sticks (Osmunda. cinnamomea), royal fern (O. regalis), the zenmai or flowering fern (O. japonica), and the vegetable fern (Athyrium esculentum). Any one of these ferns may be growing in damp woodlands of your area.

Parts used: Ferns have been used medicinally over the centuries but new concerns about carcinogens or cancer causing properties are making this a warning to consider. Most, if not all ferns, are considered poisonous to animals. Fiddleheads, as food, seem to be safe if you limit your use to the ferns mentioned above.

Because there are such a variety of ferns, I advise seeking someone with firsthand knowledge, a guide or an expert in the field of wild foods. The fiddleheads are gathered, cutting just a very few from each fern in the early spring. They are then boiled, changing the water at least twice. Reportedly, the ostrich fern is a favorite for its fine flavor. You don't have to read very far in my books to know that I always take the side of caution. I would try some, just a few, and only as a novelty.

Fireweed (Chamerion or Epilobium angustifloium): A common perennial plant that grows nearly everywhere in the Northwest except extreme arid areas. It grows in forested areas of California, Idaho, Montana, Wyoming, into Colorado, up into Canada, and on into Alaska. It can be found in the Southwest in the higher elevations such as around Flagstaff, Arizona. It is also found from the East Coast to the Midwest.

The plant becomes very distinctive looking as summer comes on. The nondescript woody stems with narrow, willow-like dark leaves erupt in vibrant pink, lavender to deep purple, spiked, 4-petal flowers. These can reach, in optimum conditions, to heights of 6 feet. Pods form atop these shoots in late summer and fall. The name has three possible derivations: 1) These wildflowers spring up first in an area that has been burned by wildfires; 2) Their appearance is like that of dancing flames erupting from the forest floor; 3) The fluff from the pods has been used as tinder for starting campfires.

Parts used: Flowers are gathered by cutting the long shoots close to the ground. Flowers and leaves can be made into a tea that acts as an over-all digestive aid, especially for colon and constipation complaints. Also acts as an anti-inflammatory and helps treat related pains inside and out. As an edible, add leaves and flowers to salads. Fireweed is one of these great plants that is very plentiful, very useful, and causes little or no adverse side effects.

Flax, Common Blue, Linseed (Linum usitatissimum) Western Flax, Wild Blue or Lewis Flax (Linum lewisii): Common flax is an annual, a refugee from Europe. Highly cultivated for the valuable seeds, used for both medicinal and non-herbal purposes (linseed oil and linen cloth). This plant has escaped from farms and gardens and can be found in many places in the U.S., growing in vacant fields and along roadsides. This year at our place a few beautiful bunches of flax invaded my property. These

seemed to be western blue flax, considered a native, and western wild blue, which grows all over the West and is not necessarily blue, but sometimes violet, pink, or yellow depending on habitat and conditions. It usually grows no higher than 1 to 2 feet. The pretty flower is delicate and graceful, looking like a dainty little sister of bachelor's button or chicory. The plain, single stems have slight, fern-like leaves. The seed pouch or fruit is round and looks a bit like a round dry pea. Inside you will find 10 small, brown, oval-shaped seeds.

Flax is considered one of the new wonder herbs, though the plant has been used for millenniums. Used as digestive aid, effective treatment for constipation and chronic bowl issues, to relieve coughs and congestion and to aid in urinary issues. It may help keep high blood pressure in check. Considered a powerful cancer fighter because of the substantial antioxidants it contains from the high content of alpha-linoleic acid.

Part used: The seed and the oil pressed from the seed.

Along the Path

    You may recall the story of Rahab and the Israelite spies, how they hid under the flax on her rooftop. She had gathered the flax there to dry. Because Rahab was willing to risk her life, the spies told her to hang a scarlet cord from her window and she would be spared when destruction came to the city. This cord was probably made from flax. Early Christians considered the blood colored cord a symbol of Christ's atonement and this story was a symbol of his coming and his willingness to pay a high price for us. More than likely the linen mentioned in the Bible was spun from flax. The fine linen cloth that the Lord Jesus was laid to rest in after his crucifixion was probably made from flax as well.

    At times, these plants are living parables to me, visible examples. I remember conducting a "Good News Club" lesson about Rahab and the scarlet chord. My wife had out the flannelgraph. Our hope was something that we might share that day would make an impression on a child about God. We were blessed in this one. That picture of the chord hanging from the window spoke to a child that day. The paper cut out prompted the child to see, and come to a better understanding, of the red blood Christ willingly shed.

Ginger, Wild (Asaruim canadense): Long-Tailed Ginger (Asarum caudatum), Hartweg's Ginger, (Asarum hartwegii) Marbled Ginger (Asarum marmoratum): There are a number of varieties of this species found across the Northern half of the U.S., up into Canada and the Alaska panhandle area. It's mostly found in damp, cool forest settings. This is our North American version of the ginger root that is commercially grown in the tropics and available at grocers. In foraging for wild ginger, look for oval to heart-shaped leaves with the distinctive ginger scent. If flowering, the tri-petal flowers are hard to see. They are usually maroon to brown and located under the much larger leaves.

On a recent sea outing to fish for rockfish off the Oregon coast, I was very glad I had ginger along. The seas were wild. The young boat captain was oblivious to all the sick customers. Acute queasiness was the order of the day for most. I had taken ginger capsules the night before and in the morning before I boarded the charter boat. Then I ate ginger cookies and sipped ginger ale. I was one of the few who didn't "chum the waters." In all honesty the urge to purge was strong but I believe it was the ginger that kept me from slipping over the edge into a miserable time of seasickness.

Great for motion sickness, even helps some pregnant women combat morning sickness. A warming herb, Ginger tea during a cold or flu may help relieve symptoms. Ginger is also considered a digestive aid, kind of like capsicum. You wonder how something that stings the taste buds and initiates perspiration can help tame the tummy, but it does.

Parts used: The leaves (highly aromatic) are steeped into tea which is used for medicinal purposes. The rhizomes, which grow horizontally just below the surface of the ground, are gathered. Be careful to take only a small portion of this slow-growing plant. The rhizomes are chopped and ground to use for seasoning teas, beverages, candies, cakes and cookies.

Susanna Reppert's Wild Ginger Dip

Here is a simple recipe to utilize the Wild Ginger you have just foraged.

½ cup sour cream
½ cup mayonnaise or plain yogurt
1 teaspoon freshly ground Wild Ginger
1 tablespoon honey
1 teaspoon grated orange peel

Combine all ingredients except orange peel. Chill at least one hour. Sprinkle grated orange peel over the top just before serving.

Grape, Wild (Vitis species): You'll need godspeed in getting to wild grapes, unless you are a lumberjack or a bear and immune to poison oak or ivy. Sometimes in damp woods you will spot woody vines with large heart shaped leaves climbing up the trees. Next you will spot the red to dark purple fruit hanging invitingly but often way over your head.

Numerous native varieties plus some naturalized ones can be found in most parts of the country. Wild grapes tend to be smaller than the cultivated versions and not nearly as sweet. But great juices, jams and jellies can be made if you can find and get to them. If you are really serious, then a pole lopper can help. Wild grapes, like cultivated ones, are high in antioxidants. Grape juice helps prevent tooth decay. Cooking oil is extracted from grape seeds, which are also used medicinally as a very effective antioxidant.

Parts used: Young leaves and fruit. The leaves can be boiled like spinach or used as a wrap for traditional Mediterranean fare.

Ground Cherry (Physalis pubescens), Chinese Lantern Plant (P. franchetii): Not a part of the cherry family at all, ground cherry is more closely related to what has become more popular in America in recent years: Tomatillo (P. ixocarpa). The name derives from the plant's growing habits, as well as the appearance of the fruit. Most varieties grow as a vine; other varieties grow upright; but none get more than a few feet tall. The leaves, which can grow up to 3 inches long, are ragged and pointed like tomato leaves. The round flower is off-white to yellow, with dark brown center. The fruit looks a bit like a green cherry. It is covered in a Chinese lantern-like husk, similar to tomatillos. In fact, one of its names is husk tomato. When ripe, its color is yellow to green. Ground cherries are ripe for eating when the husk is dry and papery. In Hawaii it is called *poha*. There are perhaps as many as 80 varieties of this plant. You'll likely find ground cherry in any except the coldest areas.

Parts used: Specifically, the delectable fruit which can be used in many ways, from jams and pastries to stews and salsas. The rest of the plant is considered toxic. The fruit is full of Vitamin A and C. Medicinally, it has been used for upper respiratory complaints and it acts as a diuretic. It is best to eat the fruit when ripe only: The unripe fruit can be toxic.

Groundnut (Apios Americana): My wife loves these sweet peanut-tasting treats. She was taught by the local natives where to find them and how to dig for them. However, the groundnut is found in much of the Midwest to the East Coast. It prefers to grow in damp areas. Out here in the West, the nut that is found is called Apos.

Various below-ground seeds or nuts are popularly called groundnut. However, Apios americana grows differently and is a perennial legume. This small vinelike plant produces edible beans above ground and edible tubers below ground. The vine grows to a few feet long. The pinnate leaves grow in groups of 5 to 7 leaflets. The small flower clusters are reddish brown. The seed pods look a bit like green beans. Below ground the stems swell, here and there, and these become what are known as the groundnut. For centuries the seeds and tubers of this plant were a major food source.

So what is it that my wife was introduced to that is called groundnut (which she eats raw)? I don't know; and I'm not eating them until I do know.

Parts used: The tubers are dug. They are half the size of an average potato. They are pealed and cooked as you would a potato. The taste is a bit like potato and turnip rolled into one. They are heavy in starch, so they have a good food value plus protein equivalent to two eggs. It has been used to make flour. Medicinally groundnut helps to stabilize blood sugars. Seed and nursery suppliers can sell you groundnut for your garden.

Caution: Groundnut is frequently found where poison ivy is prolific.

Hackberry (Celtis species): A number of varieties of this tree are indigenous to North America. The most likely ones are: American or Common Hackberry (Celtis occidentalis), found in much of the East; Western Hackberry (C. reticulate or douglasii), found in the West; and Western Hackberry as well as Desert Hackberry (C. pallida), found in the desert Southwest; Sugarberry (C. laevigata), found in the South. Hackberry is closely related to the elm family, with similar, heart-shaped leaves with serrated edges. The bark is thick and corky. The spring-blooming flowers aren't much to notice. The fruit, much sought after by animals, ranges in color from orange to purple, depending upon the variety. The desert variety is spiny with thorns that will be glad to impede your desire to pick the fruit. The fruit is usually sweet although mealy because of many seeds.

Parts used: Berries. They are a good trailside snack. If you gather enough berries, they make good jam, jelly, or syrup; they may be dried for muffins and other baked goods.

Hawthorn (Crataegus species), Yellow Hawthorn, Black Hawthorn, Western Black Haw, Douglas Hawthorn, Columbia Hawthorn, River Hawthorn, Washington Hawthorn, etc.: Hawthorn is part of the rose family and most varieties of this tree have thorns. Hawthorn grows as a bush or a small tree. Produces wonderful flowers in the spring and develops berries over the summer that look a bit like crab apples or rose hips. Birds tend to love them so humans rarely get to sample them. Most species have densely growing, rounded leaves. Will sucker quite readily.

I have taken English hawthorn berries in capsule form for years. It is this marvelous herb that sent me on this two-decade quest to understand and utilize the herbs and beneficial foods God has provided. I use hawthorn as a heart tonic and to keep my blood pressure in check. Hawthorn is considered a heart muscle repairer. Hawthorn flowers and berries are also high in antioxidants. Some studies suggests that, as well as helping the heart muscle, it may also help other weakened organs, and that it may even help with such internal injuries as hernias.

A number of varieties, that have properties similar to English hawthorn, can be found throughout the country. Some have escaped from gardens by birds carrying the seeds.

Parts used: Leaves, flowers, berries. All parts can be steeped to make a tea. Commercial tea makers use hawthorn in many tea blends. The ripe berries can be eaten fresh, but the hard seeds must be removed. May also be used for jams and jellies.

Hazelnut, American (Corylus Americana), Beaked Hazelnut (C. cornuta) and Western Hazelnut (C. cornuta californica): Hazelnut grows as a native in a number of varieties, as tall bushes up to 12 feet. Found in their native habitats in much of the East and in the West on the west side of the Sierras, the Cascades and in the coastal mountains from California to British Columbia. The leaves are somewhat heart shaped, hairy, with serrated edges. The nuts are covered in a furry sheath with a bird-like beak. American and Western pecan are covered in a wooly sheath. These nuts are usually smaller than those of commercially-grown trees.

Parts used: Nuts, eaten raw or roasted; or pulverized and used in flours.

Beaked Hazelnut

Hickory, Shagbark (Carya ovata) Carolina Hickory (C. ovata australis) Mockernut Hickory, (Carya tomentosa): This tree offers a good alternative to maple syrup, but extracted in a very different way: the syrup is made from the bark. This is a large tree growing up to 100 feet tall, found in the moist areas, river bottoms and slopes as far as the Midwest, north into Canada and as far south as Florida and Texas. Hickory is related to walnut and pecan. The leaves are divided into 5 to 7 oval, serrated leaflets. Male catkins or flowers form in the late spring in clusters of 3, up to 5 inches in length. The nuts are oval with a thick husk. The bark is light colored and shaggy thick in the more mature trees.

Mockernut is similar to the others in appearance, though some people may not think of it as hickory. The leaves are usually in 7 to 9 leaflets. The range is similar to shagbark.

Parts used: The nuts, which are sweet edibles. The bark is pulled from the tree and boiled down through a process to extract the syrup. It is available commercially.

Horseradish (Armoracea lapathifolia): Boy, can I tell you some horseradish stories. There was the time my wife mistook a scoop of mashed horseradish for mashed potatoes in a dimly-lit restaurant. She said she couldn't speak, see or hear for quite some minutes. She looked like she had been hit with a stun gun.

But horseradish in moderation sure is good and can be found in the wild. It originated in Europe and Asia and naturalized here. I am convinced horseradish roots could stretch across the U.S., from East to West. Horseradish can grow to 4 feet tall. It is coarse in appearance, with rough, serrated oval leaves. In the spring it shoots up a tall stem that develops a white flower looking a bit like broccoli gone to seed. It is related to that family of plants. The roots

are large and grow incredibly deep or will shoot out to the sides in amazing distances. Horseradish needs moisture, so look in damp areas.

Parts used: Once the leaves were used for medicinal purposes. Predominantly, the root is used for culinary purposes. It is gathered by cutting out a section. When you cut into it you will quickly realize you have the right stuff. Horseradish is used as a strong-flavored condiment, and as a digestive aid.

Horsetail (Equisetum hyemale and E. arvense): This is a singular and unique plant species that grows worldwide. It reproduces through spores and its closest relatives are ferns.

Horsetail is abundant near rivers, lakes, wetlands and moist forests across the country. Horsetail is popular with foragers. There are numerous varieties of this ancient plant.

Knowledgable foragers dig the tubers from the ground before the plant sprouts and use them as one would potatoes. E. arvense is cooked much like asparagus, when the shoots are new in early spring, right after sprouting. Scouring Rush (E. arvense), that look like little pine trees, are not edible; but, as the name suggests, have been used as a scrubbing device to clean pots and pans!

Scouring Rush

Parts used: As a food, the horsetail tubers and new shoots. In centuries past, considered a most useful herb. As a medicinal, used as an aid for digestion and kidney function, a tonic for the liver and spleen, rheumatism, prostate enlargement, neuralgia, dropsy.

High in silica which is converted to calcium. For medicinal purposes, gather and make into a tincture or tea by allowing the material to soak for a few hours. Horsetail can be found as a medicine at local health food stores.

Horsetail

Ironwood, Desert (Olneya tesota): This marvelous wood lives up to its name—tough as nails. In optimum conditions the trees can live close to 1,000 years. Evergreen, small leaved, their range is limited to the warmest parts of the Southwest, mostly the Sonoran desert. After a wet winter, ironwood trees will blossom with uncharacteristic beauty in a profusion of pink flowers. It doesn't necessarily bloom every year. From the flower a 2-inch pod develops. The 8 seeds inside, dark and hard, look like roasted coffee beans.

Parrot in an Ironwood Tree

Watch for thorns in smaller branches. Old trunks are gnarly, massive, resistant to disease and rot. They look like they have endured fire—actually, long periods with little water.

The wood is very popular for making charcoal. And if you have a powerful saw and enough carbide-tipped blades it makes for fine woodworking.

Parts used: Indigenous peoples have roasted and eaten the bitter seeds. Roasted they taste more like peanuts.

Jojoba (Simmondsia chinensis): I will be the first to admit: I am captivated by the plants of the Southwest. I guess because they are very different from the ones in the Northwest and because they grow and prosper in such harsh conditions. Also, it is fascinating to me how much benefit the natives and others have found all these plants to be.

Jojoba is one of these great plants. The fruit of the tree is edible by some people, but certainly not by all. It is the oil of the plant, used for industrial purposes, that may be its greater claim to fame. Found only in the desert Southwest, this shrubby plant grows to heights of 10 feet with an abundance of round leathery grayish green leaves reminiscent of eucalyptus. The plant produces male and female flowers. From the female flower a fruit is formed. It looks a bit like an acorn or a coffee bean. Inside are the seeds or kernels reminiscent of pine nuts. These are the edible portion, but that term is used loosely, because you could eat one and say to yourself, "This is wonderful," and the next one be spitting the sucker out!

Parts used: For use as a nut or coffee-type beverage, the preferred method is to roast them at 250° for about an hour.

For a tea, crush the raw nuts, then grind and infuse as a tea. Uniquely, this nut is 50% oil. Ladies may be familiar with jojoba as a cosmetic, skin or hair treatment. Jojoba oil has been used for many commercial purposes. Medicinally, the leaves and the infused nuts are thought to help treat swollen membranes and an array of digestive issues from the esophagus to the rectum.

Juneberries or **Serviceberries** aka Saskatoon, Shadbush and Sugarplum plus a number of other names (Amelanchier species): Here is a tasty treat to be found in almost every part of the U.S. There are 20 varieties of this plant growing in North America. Probably no other species is as well represented as this one throughout Canada and the U.S. Serviceberry trees have become popular for gardens. The names for the plant are just as fascinating as the tree or bush. The name juneberry comes from the time the fruit becomes ripe and ready to pick. It was named serviceberry because when the blossoms came out, the ground had thawed enough so that the dead could be buried and a proper "service" could be done. It was called shadberry because it bloomed when the shad fish run began.

The serviceberry shrub or tree is sun-loving woodland plant growing 10 to 20 feet tall. The trunk of the tree may grow singly or in multi-stemmed bunches. The bark is smooth and grey to grey-brown. The leaves are elliptical and lightly serrated, turning a stiking orange or red in fall. In spring the plant produces 5-petal white flowers reminiscent of apple blossoms. By summer the fruit comes on, round with a crown, reminding one of a large blueberry or huckleberry in colors from purple to red.

Parts used: Most often the fruit is very sweet when picked fresh. Unlike blueberries, there is a seed. The seed is considered edible and tastes a bit like almond. The berry is best eaten fresh or made into jams, jellies, and pies.

Serviceberry seems to be one of these wonderful plants that have been widely ignored except by the natives and the pioneers of old. It has been used medicinally for many purposes, such as a top to bottom digestive aid and a treatment for colds and flu. The juice has been used topically as ear and eye drops. Native women used a decoction of the bark to aid healing after childbirth. I don't know about you, but come this spring, this will be one of my choice fruits to seek out.

Juniper, Western Juniper, Ground Juniper (Juniperus communis, Juniperus monosperma) Rocky Mountain Juniper (Juniperus scopulorum): There are a number of varieties of this tree. Juniper ranges in most of the high desert and Great Basin lands.

I have spent many years in the high desert country of Eastern Oregon. I know the juniper tree well: its appearance, its aroma, its gnarly character and hardiness. I know the wood and have used it to build many things, from birdhouses to fences. On a cold night nothing else starts off a hot, welcoming fire in the wood stove like juniper does. It crackles and snaps and warms up a room quickly. I know the difference between a female and a male juniper tree by the abundance of blue berries that hang from the female's boughs. I have seen birds go crazy eating them. My first taste of juniper came as a seasoning in a traditionally-prepared Native American dish of salmon—the best salmon recipe I ever tasted.

There are varieties that grow in the Midwest, Eastern Canada and as far down into the south. In some places it grows in abundance where not much else will grow. The smell of the tree and of the milled lumber would remind you of cedar.

In some places juniper is considered a scourge with great efforts made to eradicate it. This is done to improve areas that once were more abundant in water before all the Juniper encroached. The grey-green prickly leaves and rough grayish to red bark are unique. Not a tall tree, with a large water supply they can grow quite stately. I don't think anything smells quite as aromatic as juniper and sagebrush after a soaking summer thunderstorm.

Parts used: For both culinary and medicinal purposes, the berries are dried. Dried berries which are being used more frequently by chefs, especially as a substitute for rosemary, which adds a similar flavor. The berries are also considered diuretic, helpful for urinary issues and may even help with the pain of gout. They have been used as a digestive aid. The extracted oil of juniper berries in a bath or humidifier can help with colds and bronchial complaints. Like echinacea, juniper may help keep you from getting a cold or the flu. Herbalists claim that having some juniper tea at the onset of either condition may help to keep it at bay or lessen its severity. But this is a strong herb; only a few dried berries should be used at any one time.

Along the Path

Job, in his lament, mentions men of dishonor that he would not even place or house with his sheep dogs. In Job 30:4 he tells of this despicable lot eating salt herbs and the root of the broom tree. Despicable perhaps; but these groups of men were good at foraging to survive.

With this in mind, what is interesting to consider is how the study, gathering and use of herbs has often been related to the occult. Such things as the casting of spells or the belief that a certain plant has a power for good or evil is evident in witchcraft and other animistic or earth worship religions.

These practices are missing the point. Here Creator God has provided so much and yet, as Romans 1:25 states, the ungodly "exchanged the truth of God for a lie, and worshipped and served created things rather than the Creator—who is forever praised." People can make gods of the earth and earthly things. But when we learn who the true God is, then we desire to use what he has provided only for purposes of good and beneficence. Our enjoyment of creation becomes praiseworthy.

Pray for those who are lost in the lie that creation/creature are somehow creator. Pray that God will open their eyes and they will see the creation for what it is and then discover the one true God for who he is.

Labrador Tea (Ledum groelandicum or also Rhododendron tomentosum) also Miner's Tea or Trapper's Tea (Ledum gladulosum): This is a far northern growing plant that you will find more into Canada and Alaska. It is to be found in the farther Northern states of the U.S. and on both northern coasts. It is found mostly in bogs and places where water is substantial. Not strictly a coastal plant, they can be found in Hells Canyon and Yellowstone.

Labrador tea was used by the natives for millenniums. It became popular in the colonies, along with bee balm and other herbs suitable for teas. During the infamous tea tax that led to the Boston Tea Party these became alternative teas. Labrador tea is related to the rhododendron family. Like them, it is an evergreen plant, growing to heights of 5 feet, with dark green leathery leaves rolled a bit on the edges. The leaf undersides are hairy and rust red. The spring blooms are white and 5-petalled, again similar to the "rhodies."

Parts used: Dried leaves are steeped in near boiling water for up to 10 minutes. As a food, it makes for a delightful, though slightly bitter beverage. As a medicinal, the tea is good for digestive issues and acts as a laxative. Strong tea can be a strong purgative. It is also beneficial in cold and flu season. This is strong stuff, not meant to be over-steeped or drank in huge quantities. A tincture is used topically for skin issues.

Lamb's Quarters (Chenopodium album), Mexican Tea or Epazote, American Wormseed (C. ambrosioides) and Strawberry Blight (C. capitatum): A wonderful plant that is very good for you. It is quite safe and grows abundantly in most places of the country. Related to Swiss chard and beets. Naturalized; not native.

A good substitute for spinach. High in vitamins and minerals. The plant grows as an annual that springs up quickly to 3 feet with abundant growth. It is upright until the heavy blooms make it bow over. Stems and leaves have a whitish appearance. Leaves are thick, reminiscent of oak leaves. Produces a profusion of small, bluish-green flowers. These produce many seeds, which are also edible.

Parts used: For best taste, harvest when young. If this weed invades your garden, gather and eat it to keep it in control. Cook the leaves and stems like spinach. Like spinach and other greens, they decrease in mass greatly when cooked, so gather large bunches. The small, black seeds are cooked as a cereal or ground into flour.

The variety, Mexican tea, is available in the South, the desert Southwest and up through the Northwest. Its leaves are used for a tea, but I would not recommend it; there are some health concerns regarding properties of this plant. Strawberry blight, a name that certainly doesn't sound inviting, is of the same family. The leaves are more triangular with irregular edges. The red fruit doesn't have much taste but is nutritious.

Lettuce, Common (Lactuca Sativa): Blue (L. floridana and L. pulchella), Hairy (L. hirsuta), Prickly (L. scariola) Wild (L. canadenisis): There are numerous varieties. A sampling of wild lettuce plants you may find in your area: Lactuca (from which we get our commercial and homegrown lettuce). A member of the daisy and chicory family. Some varieties grow as annuals, reseeding each year; others are biannuals reseeding the second year.

Prickly Lettuce

In the wild these varieties look like your salad lettuces but they may grow many feet tall with long stems and flowers. Harvest while young and tender. One variety or another grows every place in America. Some are considered native, others naturalized.

Parts used: Leaves, found early in the season before the plant begins to bolt or develop a stem and flower. The leaves are more bitter than most of our cultivated lettuces. Herbalists have used sap from the milky stems after the plant bolts, but this practice has grown out of favor by many because the medicinal results are limited.

Lily, Yellow Pond (Nuphar species) Bullhead Lily (N. variegatum) Spatterdock or Cow Lily (N. advena): There are a number of varieties of water lilies available. Some of them are good foods and beneficial herbs while some of them are deadly dangerous. Numerous varieties of the yellow pond lily are safe for consumption and grow abundantly in most parts of the country.

In still waterways look for lily colonies that have the familiar yellow round flowers with a plate-shaped stigma that sits in the center of the heart-shaped lily pad.

Parts used: The rootstalks can be cooked as you would potatoes or other starchy vegetables. As with many wild plants, changing out the water a few times is recommended. The large seeds can be fried, dried, and ground. Medicinally, the plant is a digestive aid and brings relief from digestive complaints.

Lotus, American (Nelumbo lutea and N. nucifera)): Similar in appearance but not directly related to the yellow pond lily, the American lotus can be found in places similar to the places where yellow pond lilies are found. This is a huge plant with a large yellow or white bowl-shaped flower. Hybrids of both species are also found.

Parts used: The whole plant can be consumed. Eat the engorged roots like potatoes, and the leaves like spinach.

Lovage (Ligusticum also Levisticum officinale), Celery Leaf or Parsley Leaf Lovage (L. apifolium), Gray's Lovage (L. grayi): Depending upon what expert you consult, lovage is a garden escapee brought over from Europe. Or it is a native plant. (I dunno.) Either way, this is a great plant that reminds one of celery, except it grows much bigger. Celery leaf and Gray's lovage are considered native to the Northwest. I enjoy the smell of lovage in my herb gardens. And it seems to encourage the healthy growth of other plants around it.

The seeds and leaves are the most agreeable to the palette for culinary purposes. But like celery, lovage is a great herb for treating and maintaining healthy kidney and bladder function. A diuretic, it helps with blood pressure regulation and normalization. This plant can be found most places in the U.S., depending upon variety. Lovage prefers moist, rich soils. It has long stalks, deep, divided leaves and the distinct aroma of fresh-cut celery. Can grow to 5 feet tall. At full development, the stalks bloom in white umbels like parsley and carrot, only much bigger.

Parts used: The whole plant. Leaves for culinary use; seeds for culinary and medicinal use; stalks and roots for medicinal use. Trying to use the stalks as you might celery is a disappointment; they are tough and stringy. The stems can be gathered and the essential oil pressed out. Roots and stalks, used fresh or dried, are steeped as a tea and are helpful for digestive issues but great for the kidneys and bladder. Use it topically as an antiseptic to treat wounds, scrapes and rashes.

Madrone (Arbutus menziesii) Arizona Madrone (Arbutus arizonica): In the West; this tree is related to sassafras of the East. A unique looking tree because of the bark, which is yellowish to reddish brown and is shed as new bark grows. It reminds me of someone with sunburn and the burnt skin shedding off to make way for new healthy skin. The leaves are evergreen, oblong, 3 to 6 inches in length. They individually turn brown when their life is over and do this not necessarily in fall. In

spring an abundance of white- to salmon-colored flowers turn to bunches of berries, from golden to red in color. Madrone grows on the west side of the Cascades and Sierras; the Southwest version grows in the mountains of Southern Arizona.

Parts used: Leaves are gathered for teas, berries for food. The berries taste bland and are mealy—better left for the birds. However, boiling then mashing and sweetening with honey, agave nectar or Stevia gives them a nice flavor.

Getting to the berries is the hard part; they often grow way overhead. A tea of the leaves is helpful for urinary problems if consumed in moderation and not for an extended time.

Oregon broad-leaf maple

Maple (Acer) Oregon Broad-leaf Maple (Acer macrophyllum), Red Maple (A. rubrum) and Sugar Maple (A. saccharum): I have always been curious, to the point of envy, about what it would be like to live in New England and be able to go out and collect sap from the sugar maple tree. But I am a happy westerner who is now happier because I can do the same with the Oregon broad-leaf maple tree. It grows abundantly on the western slope of the Cascades in damp woodlands and canyons.

Oregon broad-leaf maple can be found in the West from Southern California into Alaska. It prefers more of a coastal habitat, but there are groves inland near the Sierras and some isolated stands in central Idaho. The tree is characterized by huge, familiar looking three-pointed leaves and helicopter-like seed pods. Oregon broad-leaf maple trees often grow to heights of well over 50 feet and to diameters of nearly 2 feet.

Red maple and sugar maple trees are indigenous to the East, from North to South.

Parts used: The gathered sap. There are some real benefits to using the sap, which is usually made into syrup. One is the cost factor. Have you seen the price on a bottle of real maple syrup? I understand why it is so expensive; it takes many gallons of sap reduced down to make one gallon of syrup. Nevertheless, it is certainly a better alternative than our modern sugar-laden, high-fructose syrups.

Best gathering for the sap is in spring before the tree begins to bud. Pick a day that has warmed up quite a bit compared to the still-chilly nights. Sap begins to move up the branches preparing to bud. When the sap is really running you may even notice that it oozes from the leaves. At the base of the tree and on the sunny side, with enough room to hang a bucket, a shallow hole is drilled no more than 2 inches across. Then a metal or plastic tube or straw is inserted 1 to 2 inches deep. The diameter should be ¾ inch. If you have picked the right tree and the right time, soon you will be rewarded with free flowing sap. It takes patience, but as much as a gallon can be had in 4 to 6 hours.

Once gathered, the sap is poured into a pan and heated to 160° or until the liquid begins to steam. Then, watching carefully, reduce the sap to syrup. If you are out in the late spring when the flowers have bloomed, they make a sweet addition to salads; or you could make maple flower petal jelly or jam.

Herbal benefits: First, the pure syrup is a good source for manganese and zinc. Manganese can act as an antioxidant and zinc helps the immune system and is good for the heart. Zinc also helps a man's prostate stay healthy. While this sap is certainly sugar, it has not been through a refining process which takes out the health benefits. But remember, a little bit of this sweetener goes a long way.

Mesquite (Prosopis species) Honey Mesquite (P. glandulosa), Screwbean Mesquite (P. pubescens) and Velvet Mesquite (P. velutina): A true multipurpose plant. Its range is the deserts of the Sonoran, Mojave and Chihuahua. It can be found as far east as Texas, into the far south part of Utah and west into Southeastern California. This wonderful plant has served natives and immigrants as food, medicine, and multipurpose utility. A number of varieties exist. It grows as a small tree, at best. Deciduous, very hardy and drought tolerant. The tap root is often many times longer than the above-ground tree itself. The leaves are narrow and feathery, and I think very attractive. Like many of its desert-dwelling neighbors, young mesquites produce thorns sharp enough to penetrate a boot. I have extracted them from boot and foot. The wood is hard, great for woodworking if you have a saw sharp enough. Mesquite produces a legume or pod, enjoyed by beast and man alike.

Parts used: As a food, the pods. Called *pechitas*, these "beans" provide a great protein and starch staple. The golden sap or pitch is sweet. As a treat it is eaten as a candy; medicinally it is used for the treatment of cold and flu symptoms. The flowers are some of the finest for honey and are edible. If you choose to sample the flowers, check carefully—there may be a bug in there. The pods can be dried and ground into flour and added to other grain flours. We had some wonderful mesquite cookies with no sugar added, and found them very flavorful; we could not eat just one.

Medicinally, the roots, bark and leaves are used topically as eyewash for pinkeye, and to treat acne and dandruff. Use it internally as a tea to kill parasites in the intestines. And of course any BBQ-loving fellow can tell you, mesquite makes a great smoke for meat.

Along the Path

I like the maple leaf's pretty distinctiveness. It seems that God has created many of the leaves and flowers in a way that will remind us of him if we are observing. So when you look at the leaf, you will notice a great representation of the trinity of God; Father, Son and Holy Spirit. At the top, the three points are distinct; yet, at the bottom they are one. We can see one-in-three and three-in-one, the way our God operates. I am reminded of a praise song that has been sung for years that you are probably familiar with. The chorus starts with, "The trees of the field will clap their hands" (leaves, I assume). This comes from Isaiah 55:12: "You will go out in joy, and be led forth in peace; the mountains and hills will bust into song before you, and all the trees of the field will clap their hands." This is part of a long description about the new Zion, our heavenly home, and the joy we will experience. We can experience that joy a bit now.

I love to be out in God's creation much more than in the towns and cities that man has made. When you go a gathering go out with joy—not just happiness, but the joy the Lord gives. If you listen closely, I think you will hear the hills and mountains burst into song. And if there is a breeze accompanying this song of creation, then you will probably hear the trees keeping time with their "hands."

Milkthistle (Silybyum or Carduus marianum): This is a very important medicinal herb for those who have had liver damage, especially if it was brought on by alcohol consumption and abuse. When you consider that alcohol consumption and addiction are the number one drug problem in America, the need for this is even more acute. Milkthistle has been naturalized and grows wild in the West more to the coastal side, mountains and valleys west of the Sierras and Cascades. Reportedly it has been found in Idaho and in Utah. But there are a lot of thistle plants out there that are not milkthistle, it being the rarer of the genus.

If you are truly motivated to forage for this plant, you may want to contact your local wildflower society and see if they can help you identify it from the rest of the tribe. The plant is identified by of the milky sap that the stalk emits. Seeds are used medicinally.

Milkthistle is a tall, rangy plant reaching heights of 6 feet or more if the conditions are right. It is a thorny mess that will defend its life from being picked. The flower, one to a stem, is a typical thistle flower, pink to violet in color. The seeds form late in the season and are brown in color, ½ inch long and shiny.

Parts used: To collect these things you need a certain amount of bravery and just the right equipment to amputate the flower head from the stalk. Then the seeds are extracted carefully from the hairy mass that makes up the flowers. Seeds are used either fresh or dried and specifically for the treatment of an injured liver. Fortunately, you can find milk thistle in capsule form at your health food stores. Milkthistle seed has been used for millenniums, a truly effective treatment for the liver.

Milkweed, Common (Asclepias syriaca), Desert Milkweed (Asclepias erosa, A. subulata & A. albicans) Narrow-leaved Milkweed (A. fascicularis) Showy Milkweed (A. speciosa): After reading about how hard and painful it might be to get Milk Thistle, here is something that is much easier and just as wonderful. Common Milkweed is distributed through much of the East and into the Midwest, growing happily in sunny areas.

The plant gets its name from the milky sap known as latex that is found when the stems are broken. The young plant can also be distinguished by downy hairs or floss. The natives would use this, along with the fibers of the plant stems to make textiles. The plant can grow to heights of 5 feet. The roots prefer a sandy or loamy soil and may grow underground to 12 feet deep. The leaves are large and downy underneath. The flowers form in the second year and grow in clusters or umbels with colors from white to violet. The seed pods are rough and brownish. The plant is considered very toxic to livestock who eat it raw. However, for humans, after proper preparation, it is safe for consumption.

Caution: Milkweed can be easily confused with toxic hemp dogbane. The main difference is there are none of the downy hairs upon the plant. This is a plant that you must be careful with regarding its use as an edible and as a medicinal.

Milkweed is used more and more in flowers gardens by those who wish to attract butterflies especially monarchs.

Desert milkweed is found in three varieties, albicans and erosa looking very similar to common milkweed while subulata hardly looks like milkweed at all and is described by noted herbalist Michael Moore as "a big bundle of sticks" with small, pale white- to cream-colored flowers. These plants can be found in the deserts of Southern California such as around Palm Springs, into Southern Nevada, Southern Utah, and Arizona and in some of the desert areas of Colorado. In the Northwest and into Northern California narrow-leaved milkweed and showy milkweed can be found.

Common Milkweed

Parts used: Pretty much the whole plant for different purposes. The shoots, new leaves, flower buds and immature fruit are eaten, but must be thoroughly cooked in boiling water with a number of water changes. The boiling process also changes what is pretty bitter to a more palatable taste.

The steeped, dried rootstalk is used as a tea. It is used for the treatment of colds and other respiratory concerns, as a digestive aid, and as a diuretic. It is gathered in the fall and winter. The sap can be used topically to treat warts. The floss is considered a great alternative to wool because it is much lighter and yet keeps one warmer. It is used for everything from pillows to life preservers.

Miner's Lettuce, Siberian or Candy Flower (Claytonia sibirica), Miner's Lettuce (C. perfoliata): An annual related to purslane. Found in much of the West. A short-lived annual that reseeds. Not a true lettuce, but really tasty, fresh in spring. Miner's lettuce grows more abundantly east and west of the Cascades; Siberian miner's lettuce, or candy flower, grows more west of the Cascades, though it can be found in canyons and forested locales east of the Cascades.

The basal leaves of miner's lettuce are oval to round, bright green, in twos opposite the white to pink flowers. Siberian lettuce leaves are more heart-shaped, green to bronze, and the flowers are striped, abundant, and white to pinkish white, with a candy stripe appearance. This small plant usually grows no taller than a foot.

Parts used: The stems and leaves, long consumed by natives and immigrants as a nice spring salad or lightly cooked pot herb. Roots can be cooked and are considered tasty.

Mint, Brook or Field (Mentha Arvensis); Also Peppermint, Spearmint, Bergamot, European Pennyroyal: Rarely a day that goes by that I don't use mint in some way.

My wife and I get excited when we are following a stream, usually fishing pole in hand, and smell the sweet scent of mint. We look down to see that we are trodding on the plants. Brook mint is considered North America's only true native mint, all others having come across the sea aboard ship with explorers and settlers. That doesn't mean you can't find other mints such as peppermint and spearmint in wild settings.

Brook mint is sweet and mild, lighter in color and smaller in size than our domesticated mints. Brook mint can be found in most places where water flows in creeks and rivers, and around lakes and reservoirs. The flowers form on the stems from top to bottom rather than just the top like other mints. Brook mint contains ample menthol, making it a treasure. It is the most flavorful and mild of the mint family.

Mountain mint, found in the Midwest to the East, tends to grow more as garden mints grow. You will notice a stronger aroma and taste.

Bergamot mint is sometimes called lemon mint (Mentha cirtrata). In the West, bergamot mint is found along the coast, coast ranges and on the west side of the wet valleys of the Willamette. It has large flower heads. The large leaves are a favorable addition to tea mixes.

Peppermint and spearmint are escapees from the gardens and cultivated fields. Both can be found in most places in the Northwest and into Northern and Central California.

European pennyroyal is another escapee. This smallish plant is dependent upon water for size. It has a very pungent odor that is nearly disagreeable. We have found great amounts of it west of the Cascades. It is considered a bane by ranchers and farmers because it is invasive and a danger to farm animals. It has had a reputation for causing women to abort pregnancies, planned or not. It does have some good medicinal properties, but should only be administered by well-trained herbalists.

Pennyroyal

Gather mint in the wild the same way you would from your garden, cutting the stems about halfway down so that the leaves you get are new and clean. Dry it in a cool place without direct sunlight. I dry much of my herbs on my back deck, safe from direct sun yet with good airflow. Mints are first a stomach tonic, good for your whole digestive tract.

Use for jellies; smallest leaves in salads and desserts. A good rule of thumb: When out searching for mint, you'll likely find it. Regardless of variety, those mints found in areas of some shade and abundant water will have the best taste.

Wild Peppermint

Along the Path

Brook mint reminds me of the Bible verse found in Psalms 1:3. "He is like a tree planted by streams of water, which yields its fruit in season and whose leaf does not wither. Whatever he does prospers." Our lives, with roots planted deeply next to the living water of God should be sweet, lush and plentiful. Our Christian lives are automatically prosperous lives if we stay close to the living water and true bread that God is for us. This prosperity, however, may look different. It may not be a big house in a fancy neighborhood with all the trappings to boot. Our prosperity in the Lord is seen in how—and to what extent—we touch others with the love of God. I like the little clue to this that Proverbs 11:10 states: "When the righteous prosper, the city rejoices." Our prosperous Christian lives will result in many people being touched.

Mormon Tea, Cowboy Tea, Mexican Tea and a lot of other names (Ephedra aspera, E. californica and E. trifurca): This common plant of the West has been used for millenniums by indigenous peoples of America, and by pioneers, as a beverage to stimulate and refresh, similar to that first cup of morning coffee. However, as you may recall, ephedrine came under great scrutiny by the FDA because of lethal side effects; people were dying from the use of it. Ephedrine comes from a large family of plants, and much of what was used, but is now illegal in this country, came from China. Mormon tea plants are identified by their appearance, like little pine or fir trees growing as shrubs that usually grow no taller than four feet. They even have little cones that look like monkey paws.

They range mostly in the western states, except the northwestern states of Washington, Idaho, Montana and Wyoming. Mormon tea is related to the ephedrine genus. Ephedrine increases heart rate and blood pressure so obviously is dangerous to people with those conditions. The native plants of the West purportedly contain less or none of the ephedrine alkaloid compared to those of Asia. Ephedrine has other medicinal uses; it has been used for the treatment of cold and flu symptoms.

Parts used: The branches, brewed as a tea. A cautionary note: Ephedrine can certainly be dangerous; it wasn't banned for nothing. Research seems to indicate that the varieties of the ephedrine family that grow in the states contain little or none of this alkaloid. Nevertheless, good or bad, safe or dangerous, people who drink it find it refreshing—and yes, stimulating.

Mountain Ash, American (Pyrus americana) Northern Mountain Ash (P. decora) Cascade Mountain Ash (Sorbus scopulina): An attractive small tree or large shrub, depending upon variety and location. The leaves are fine toothed, lance shaped and compound. In the spring white clusters of flowers appear. These turn to red or orange fruit in the late summer and fall. Cascade mountain ash is found in the Northwest and eastward to the Rockies. American mountain and northern mountain are found along the northern East Coast and as far down as Georgia. The fall berries are very distinct and attractive to animals.

Parts used: We humans would find the berries bitter of taste, but cooking and freezing improves the flavor. If you are looking for a tart jam or jelly, these will do, and they are full of pectin. The berries are of medicinal value and have been used to treat diabetes, scurvy, kidney issues, and as a blood tonic.

Mulberry, Red (Morus rubra) White Mulberry (Morus alba), Texas Mulberry (M. microphylla): Do you remember the old nursery rhyme song, "Here we go 'round the mulberry bush, the mulberry bush . . ."? When I discover bushes of these delectable berries, I do not go around them—I stop and pick some. I am mindful, though, to consume them carefully. Native mulberry bushes grow from the East to the Midwest and in the South as far west as Texas. Mulberry is cultivated in many places, so to find a stray one elsewhere would not be a surprise. Mulberry bushes can exceed 50 feet in height. The serrated leaves may grow oval or 2- or 3-lobed. The fruit is the most distinguishable part, looking like an elongated blackberry or boysenberry, and growing in multiples instead of singly. The fruit is very sweet; but it is important to eat it only when ripe.

Parts used: Berries, best cooked for jams, jellies and such.

Warning: There are concerns that the unripe berries and the shoots are hallucinogenic.

Mullein, Common (Verbascum thapsus): This has to be one of the most common plants in North America and yet one of the most unusual in appearance. It is stately yet homely, defying easy description. Common mullein grows just about everywhere. In fact, you may not have to go out in the wild to see it; it may sprout up in your yard as if overnight. Suddenly you notice there are these broad, fuzzy leaves hugging at the ground. If you let it go the first year, then in the next year it will shoot up a long stalk, perhaps as tall as 8 feet. From there, heads of tiny yellow flowers sprout looking somewhat like a corncob exposed, with the husk pulled.

There are hundreds of varieties of this plant but the one that is most common and likely to be seen is the Verbascum thapsus. It has many other names and is steeped in history and myth. This plant is also known as Aaron's staff, bunny's ear, flannel leaf, candlewick plant and hag taper. A number of other species have been developed for showy flowers in the garden. In the wild, and more likely towards the coast, you could find moth mullein. These also are tall plants, but with branches and larger yellow flowers than common mullein.

Parts used: In days of old, it is said, the stems were dipped in tallow to make candles or torches, and the downy leaves used for lamp wicks.

Mullein has been given both mythic and occultic aspects. One of its alternative names is hag taper. Hag is another name for witch. In Bible times King Agrippa believed the fragrance of the plant could overpower demons.

While it may be quite common, I like to think God gave it to us, because it is so prolific and available in so many places and has a number of herbal advantages.

Utilizing the leaves, flowers, and even the roots to make into a tea, it has long been used to treat colds and respiratory complaints and as a digestive aid. The tea may be so powerful as to have anti-viral properties. The flowers have been used as a hair dye by women who would like to be a little blonder (I won't comment on that).

If you want to try it as a tea, stick with the flowers, well strained, and see what you think.

Mullein likes sun and seems to prefer poor soil. It is very drought tolerant, seemingly able to grow and prosper on very little water. We took a hike recently on a gravel path that had been converted from a railroad track. In bare and sunny spots the mullein was everywhere, as if enjoying a meander down the "rails to trails" walking path.

Along the Path

My favorite alternate name for the mullein plant is "Aaron's staff." As you may recall, God provided a staff for Aaron—evidently made from an almond branch, though. My son-in-law made me a staff and even carved on it, "Pa's Walking Stick." I use it to negotiate trails and move things out of my way; and if needed, I could use it as a defensive weapon. I am not sure how mullein came to be called "Aaron's staff"; that story is lost to antiquity. I can imagine, though, a person familiar with the story of the budding of Aaron's staff may have noticed one day that the bare spike of the mullein had budded and blossomed yellow flowers. Read Aaron's story for yourself in Numbers 17.

Rods or staffs, in Bible days, were very important; most every person would have had one. The main mode of transportation was walking, so the staff's main purpose was walking stick. If it had a crook on one end, then it could also serve to handle sheep and goats. It could be a rod of discipline for errant children or adults. Symbolically the purpose of the budding of Aaron's rod was to denote power, authority and the promise of God to do what he says he will do; it demonstrates that he has the power and authority to carry out his promises and purposes.

Our promise in Psalm 23 is that God's rod and staff are there as a comfort to us. With them he will direct us and lovingly discipline us; and he will use them as weapons to keep the enemy from harming us.

Nettle, Stinging (Urtica dioca and Urtica urens) plus numerous varieties: My first experience with this herb was less than positive. I had little familiarity with it, when, near the Upper Klamath Lake, I saw what looked like spearmint growing in abundance. I grabbed a few leaves off a plant and held it up to my nose expecting to sniff the rich scent of mint. But no pungent sweetness greeted my nose. Instead, I thought I had grabbed some leaves with a hornet attached and that the angry insect had somehow stung my nose, upper lip, and fingers.

My lips swelled and my nose and fingers felt full of slivers. I had tangled with stinging nettle! Some time later I finally came to terms with the fact that there are great benefits to this herb if one treats it with respect. I was reminded of the statement God makes in Genesis 3:17-18, after Adam and Eve fell from grace: "Cursed is the ground because of you. . . . It will produce thorns and thistles for you."

God's perfect creation was up-ended by sin. Even some of the plants, while still beneficial as food and medicine, could do you harm. This is important to understand, especially when you go out gathering. Certain plants will make you sick; some will kill you.

Well, I can't tell you how stupid I felt for getting tangled with the nettle; an herbalist like me should know better, right? So I have taken some comfort in knowing that other herbalists, some much more knowledgeable than I, have done the same thing.

Nettle won't kill you, but improper contact will always be remembered. When looking for stinging nettle, look for something similar to the long spiky, serrated leaves of spearmint. Your first clue is that if it is mint, you will smell it, especially on a sunny day when oil is flowing. If not, it may be nettle. Nettle is found pretty much everywhere, sometimes in huge colonies, along waterways, wetlands, and in ditches. Best gathered in the spring, and with sturdy gloves, long-sleeves, long pants, and boots for protection.

Parts used: Medicinally, the juice is used. For an edible, the young shoots and leaves. Commercially, capsules are made from the juice to help treat urinary and prostate issues. After my initial experience, I decided that I should give the plant another chance, sort of, so I bought capsules. The bottle sat unopened for weeks before I gained the courage to try it. Remembering the angry welts, I thought, "If it felt like that on the outside, what is going to happen to my insides?" I imagined the feeling of urinating fire, but that didn't happen. All kidding aside, the juice is a great digestive aid and treatment for urinary concerns similar to the effects of cranberry juice. Stinging nettle is also useful as a diuretic. The leaves and young shoots, boiled for 10 minutes, can be utilized as a tea or added to soups and stews as you would add any vegetable.

New Jersey Tea or Red Root (Ceanothus americanus): This low bushy shrub grows in the East up into Canada, south into Florida, and as far west as Texas. It makes an excellent tea, brewed in the same way you would camelia sinsetheis or green or black tea. The New Jersey tea bush is low growing with heart-shaped serrated leaves that may remind you of sunflower leaves. From June to August, puffy white flowers appear, made up of many tiny petals growing at the top of long stalks. It has a red stalk and root, hence one of its names.

Parts used: Leaves and root for tea, both edible and medicinal. The root is considered a tonic for the spleen and a digestive aid for a number of complaints.

Oak (Quercus species): This is a family of trees with many species. They can be grouped into four distinct categories: Red Oak, White Oak, Black Oak and Live Oak. Nearly every state in the U.S. has representatives of these common trees. Red, White, and Black Oak leaves are the most familiar, with their 6- to 8-leaf lobes per dark green leaf and, of course, acorns. All acorns are edible, but the acorns of the white

oak are considered the most favorable. Live oaks, which tend to grow in the southern states and in warmer climates in the North, keep their leaves. These are more oval without the lobes. The tree sheds year round as leaves die off individually. The chestnut oak leaf is oval, with a pointed tip and more of a serrated edge. Acorns wear a cap when hanging on the trees. The shells are cracked and the nut inside is eaten. The emery oak (Q. emoyi) of the Southwest is said to have the sweetest acorn. The bark is also utilized as a medicinal.

Parts used: Nuts of the acorn, from certain species of the white oak, are edible right out of the shell. To enjoy the maximum flavor of the nuts, which are high in tannin, they are boiled in successive changes of water until the water stays clear. The nuts can also be ground to meal and used for flour. Nuts and bark are gathered in spring. Young branches, twigs, and bark that is thin on the trunk can be brewed as a decoction and used for a variety of conditions, from digestive issues, upper respiratory complaints, painful menstrual cycles, urinary issues, and even as a mouth and throat gargle. You can make a decoction of one ounce of bark to one quart of water, boiling it down to a pint.

Ocean plants: Dulce (Rhodymenia palmata), Glasswort (Salicornia species), Irish Moss (Chondrus crispus), Edible Kelp (Alaria species), Sea Lettuce (Ulva lactuca): There are an amazing variety of ocean plants that are edible and beneficial. In fact, you might be surprised at how much you have already consumed without knowing it, from fillers in prepared foods to cosmetics, skin and hair care products. On our Oregon Coast, long tube-like plants called kelp can be found dislodged from the ocean and strewn over the shore. So what do we do, take home that slimy thing, chop it and stir fry it?

One way to begin to consider edible seaweed is to make a paradigm shift in our thinking and begin to call the plants "sea vegetables and ocean herbs." First, ocean plants are algae taking on many shapes, colors and forms. They also tend to be high in iodine, many vitamins and minerals. Some have such great medicinal benefit, that they are used to treat a number of complaints and conditions. These plants are gathered as they grow fresh or where just dislodged, like kelp.

Dulce is a far northern plant that grows from the Jersey shore through New England and is much more prolific in Canada. Dulce grows in dark red to purple fan-shaped fronds to a height of one foot and can be found around rocks and structures at low tide. The leaves can be eaten raw but are best boiled and used in many dishes.

Glasswort is more likely to be found in estuaries where the salt and fresh water mix during high and low tide. It can be found in alkaline flats on both the East and West coast. This perennial looks like a succulent with slender branches that give the appearance of pickles. The plant sprouts tiny pink flowers. The crunchy, salty stems can be eaten like you might a pickle. It is called pickleweed for that reason.

Irish moss has a brackish appearance with flat, forked fronds. Red or green in color, this small plant is less than a foot tall. It grows along the Atlantic coast down to the Carolinas and has been found on the Pacific coast in California. It grows in huge dense colonies. The plant has much mucilage and when the mid rib and fronds are cooked it exudes a gelatin matter. Commercially it is gathered and used for many food fillers. See, I mentioned that you have probably eaten and used ocean plants more than you realized. You can cook it, adding it to a soup or other dishes. It is rich in protein and minerals but quite tasteless.

Kelp

Edible kelp, the one that grows more on the North Atlantic, can be eaten utilizing the small lower fronds, raw or cooked as a vegetable. Only eat what is very fresh.

Sea lettuce looks like its name, green with wide leaves growing to nearly 2 feet tall. Found on both coasts, its name suggests its use. Might make for a wonderful addition to crab or shrimp Louie.

Perhaps we are missing out on wonderful food sources by not considering the many sea vegetables and ocean herbs God has provided for us.

Along the Path

Jonah found himself wrapped in seaweed just before the Lord provided a big fish to save his life and teach him a lesson about obedience. Always in movement, the sea is a symbolic description of our lives corporately. We are a restless and an in-flux creation. If you have ever spent time on a stormy sea then you know it is exhausting as you try to keep your balance. You are always being required to move and adjust; and the voyage will just plain wear you out. This is a parabolic example, or a good picture, for us to consider and remember. Our disobedience to God is like being tossed about on the seas. Better to find safe harbor with God in our willingness for obedience. "But the wicked are like the tossing sea, which cannot rest, whose waves cast up mire and mud. '"There is no peace,' says my God, 'for the wicked.'" Isaiah 57:20-21

Ocotillo (Fonquieria splendens): Most of the year this thorny plant looks more dead than alive. Ocotillo looks like a pile of upright, extremely thorny spikes growing to 20 feet tall. This unique plant grows north of the U.S./Mexico border. It is not a true cactus, but rather a distant cousin.

The plant's range is only throughout the desert southwest. If there is enough winter precipitation, then in the spring—wow, is it ever beautiful! Ocotillo puts on a show with an incredible array of red flowers. Along with the blooms, there comes a luxurious leaf sprout, though some years the flowers make their appearance first. One moment the plant looks dead. In a matter of days, or seemingly overnight, it becomes one of the liveliest plants of the desert. Looking like florescent red tubes, the flowers are soon occupied by hummingbirds and other nectar-seeking creatures.

Parts used: Humans also can sample the flowers by sucking deeply on the petals to get out a sweetness that some say is beyond delicious. If you can get enough without being too punctured, fill your sun tea pitcher with the blossoms. Set it out in the hot sun for an hour, then enjoy a refreshing, tart tea.

As a medicinal, use roots and bark. Fresh bark, gathered with much care and from the center of the plant, is cut out in 4- to 6-foot sections. The tincture made from the bark is said to be helpful for women's reproductive issues as well as prostate issues for men. It has also been used to help treat mild urinary problems. Natives used tea from the roots to treat a host of problems, from coughs to a soak for tired and sore muscles.

The root word of "ocotillo" means "ocote" or "torch" as in the appearance of the rare bloom. In a visit to Tumucacori Mission in Tubac, Arizona we noticed aboriginal housing built with ocotillo sticks for walls and roof. They also make a good fence; the thousands of barbs help to keep in what needs to stay in, and out what needs to stay out.

Organ Pipe Cactus: See Cactus

Paloverde, Blue (Parkinsonia florida), Foothills Paloverde (P. micophylla) and Mexican Paloverde (P. piaculeata): A very common tree of the desert Southwest. Paloverde means green pole. The tree, bark, and leaves are green. When I escape from the Northwest's brown, gray winter to Arizona in January, it is nice to see something so green, even in the parched desert. The tree is unique in that the process of photosynthesis takes place through the bark as well. With adequate moisture, spring flowers offer an array of yellow that brightly transforms the desert. All varieties of these hardy, easy-to-grow trees are used as ornamentals.

Parts used: Paloverde produces large seed pods with edible seeds. Though plentiful, they're not the most delicious food of the desert. Roast the seeds; the raw seeds are considered toxic. Grind them to meal for use in baking or make (wild tasting) porridge.

Passionflower (Passiflora mexicana, P. foetida, P. incarnata & P. tenuiloba): One of my all-time favorite flowers. I like the unique bloom, its potency as an herbal medicinal, and its spiritual aspect. The passionflower may be one of the best symbols of the physical, emotional and spiritual life that God provides for us.

Grows as a vine with at least 3 varieties native or naturalized to North America. Most are considered tropical or subtropical, growing naturally in the extreme southern parts of the U.S. The incomparable flower makes this plant unique. Considered symbolic of Christ's Passion, the flower consists of 5 sepals and petals, a hairy fringe coming from the calyx, a small stalk of a pistil from which 3 stigmas protrude, and 5 stems. All these in an array of colors from purple to green, white, or beige.

The native Mexican passionflower ranges only in the southern tips of Arizona, New Mexico and parts of southern Texas.

Famed Southwest herbalist Michael Moore talks about finding passionflowers in desolate desert hideaways and also in cluttered back alleys of L.A., Tucson, Albuquerque and Las Vegas. Passiflora incarnata is a naturalized plant in many places of the Southeast.

Parts used: The whole plant can be utilized. The flowers can also be eaten (although it seems a little like desecration to me). I use passionflower regularly as a tea or in capsule form. I use it as a nerve aid for the permanently pinched and inflamed nerves in my back. Along with a combination of hops, valerian, chamomile and other herbs, it is one of the very few medicinal helps that I have found to keep this painful business at bay. Passionflower acts as a sedative on many parts of the body, able to calm down pulse, respiration, normalize blood pressure, aid the digestive system, help with a woman's monthly aches and pains, and calm the mind. It is also quite safe when using recommended doses. The fruit is also edible; it is available in the late summer to fall, and it is very tasty.

Pawpaw (Asimina triloba) aka Poor Man's Banana: Unique to the U.S., and there are a number of varieties of it. It holds the unique distinction of being the largest native fruit in the country. People living in the South and the East are most familiar with pawpaw.

This is truly a wondrous fruit. Much research is being done concerning its medicinal potential. Pawpaw's natural range is the temperate woodlands of the East. It is also found as far west as Iowa and south to Florida and Texas. It has been cultivated across the country and does well in some parts of the West. A deciduous tree, it grows up to 20 feet as an understory tree. The dark green oval to oblong leaves grow up to a foot long. The flower buds are dark brown producing purplish, 3-petal flowers that grow upside down, early to late spring. Each bloom can produce multiple fruits.

The fruit, which grows in clusters, looks a bit like an over-ripe banana. It can be quite large, weighing over a pound. It ripens mid August to October. Usually picked green and allowed to ripen. The taste is described as that of fine custard. The pawpaw's total appearance—leaves, flowers and fruit—reminds one of the tropical plant, papaya, from which the name "pawpaw" may have derived.

Parts used: The fruit, which has a very short shelf life. It can be dehydrated or made into jams and jellies. I know of folks in West Virginia who make banana nut cake using this "American banana." Natives have used the seeds medicinally. Seeds have been ground and used as an insecticidal in the treatment of lice. There are now commercially made shampoos with pawpaw extract. Intriguing research is being done on pawpaw because of its potential to reduce cancerous tumors. Acetogenins extracted from the twigs has proved helpful in combating Leukemia, and prostate and lung tumors. Another wondrous plant that nourishes and heals.

Pecan (Carya illinoensis): This tree is native to the Midwest and the Deep South and is cultivated in the Southwest. This is a large-growing tree similar in appearance to walnut and considered a species of hickory. It has dark brown bark and the toothed narrow leaves grow in leaflets of 9 or more. The nuts grow in groups of four. The name "pecan" seems to come from an Algonquian word meaning to crack with a stone. To get one of these open is a task, but well worth it.

Parts used: The nut, which has a buttery flavor. High in protein, unsaturated fats and Omega 6. And who can refuse a slice of pecan pie?

Green pecans in tree

Pennycress, Field (Thlaspi arvense): Named after the shape of the seed pods. This is a naturalized plant to the U.S., including some 60 varieties, and is part of the mustard family. Field pennycress is an introduced plant with a range now encompassing most of North America. One of the most prolific and widespread naturalized weeds. It has food and medicinal value, but that comes with a warning.

The leaves are long, narrow and lobed. The seed pods are penny shaped, oval and flat. The seed is deeply notched. Pennycress grows from 12 to 30 inches tall. An annual, or occasionally biannual. The plant flowers at the top with the fruit or penny shaped seeds below. The small, white flowers grow in a round cluster. The flowers are scentless, but the leaves give off a mustard/garlic aroma.

Parts used: Leaves and seed pods can be used in salads or cooked as greens. As a medicinal, the plant has been used as an anti-inflammatory and a blood tonic. It has been used for treating colds, flu, and fever. There is interest in using this plant as a bio fuel.

Warning: There are concerns about toxicity. The plant contains significant amounts of Glucosinolates. This is mainly a problem for cattle, who may ingest large quantities.

Peppergrass or Pepperweed (Lepidium species) Field Peppergrass or Poor Man's Peppergrass (L. campstere & L. virginicum): Part of the mustard family of plants, peppergrasses make up a large group of species. Peppergrass, of one species or another considered common weeds, are found just about everywhere. Depending upon what source you read, it is considered a native plant or a naturalized plant. In the spring look for long basal, serrated leaves and long stems to 18 inches. As the season progresses, clusters of 4-petal flowers appear, usually white with yellow anther. Later, flattish, oval pods develop. The leaves have a strong aroma of pepper.

Parts used: Like mustard, it is used for its peppery tasting leaves and seeds eaten and cooked like mustard. The leaves are full of vitamins, iron and other nutrients so it makes a fine green for consumption.

Virginia Pepperweed

Alkali Pepperweed

Persimmon (Diospyros virginiana): This unique fruit. It grows as a native in the South, Midwest and into lower New England. It is cultivated in California and elsewhere. The trees with their ebony bark grow to 60 feet. The leaves are oval, pointed on the end and dark green and glossy on top. The fruit is peach shaped but smaller. When ripe it is orange to purplish-red in color. The trees look striking in fall after they lose their leaves and bright orange fruit still clings. If fruit is eaten unripe it is very tart. Pick them firm and let them ripen to glossy softness, and they are very sweet and tasty.

Parts used: The fruit eaten fresh but also used for many other recipes. The leaves are said to make a delightful tea which is full of Vitamin C.

Maureen Rogers' Persimmon Cookies

½ cup butter
1 cup sugar
1 egg
1 teaspoon baking soda
1 cup persimmon pulp
2 cups flour
⅛ teaspoon salt
¼ teaspoon cloves
½ teaspoon mace
1 cup raisins
1 cup chopped pecans

In the bowl of an electric mixer, cream the butter with the sugar until mixture is fluffy. Beat in the egg. Add baking soda to the persimmon pulp, then add to the creamed mixture. Sift together the flour, salt and spices. Add to the creamed mixture in three portions, beating well after each addition. With a mixing spoon, blend in raisins and nuts. Drop dough by teaspoonfuls onto a greased cookie sheet, flattening each cookie to the desire shape because these cookies do not spread much during baking. Bake 12-15 minutes in a 350°F oven, testing with a toothpick to determine when done. Makes 30 cookies.

Along the Path

While on duty as a Salvation Army officer I was helping out in Missouri during the devastating flooding of the Mississippi and Missouri Rivers. The damage was incredible and many people were displaced.

We traveled around in an RV providing aid and comfort for the people who were victims of the flooding. We found these folks gracious and patient beyond belief and happy for what ever help could be provided.

Once we were invited into some elderly folks' flood-ravaged home. The water had nearly filled the bottom half of the house. Now they were trying to live in it although the conditions were unsafe. We wanted to find out what we could do to help. The lady of the house, with gracious southern hospitality, wanted to serve something even though there was little to serve.

She had scavenged some persimmons and asked if I'd like one. I didn't think I would—they looked overripe; but I certainly didn't want to turn her down. I had never eaten a persimmon before. But I ate one this time. And I will say this: Her hospitality was much sweeter than that fruit. It was definitely not overripe.

I believe that hospitality is one of the fruits of the Spirit. Whether all of us have that gift or not, Paul instructs us in Romans 12:13 that we are to "practice hospitality." In Romans 16:23 he identifies a person named Gaius. We know little of who this person was; but Paul was so struck by this person that he states "whose hospitality I and the whole church here enjoy." Our hospitality becomes an enjoyment for others. We are to remember that it is "more blessed to give than to receive." Then we find a blessed enjoyment as well.

You might meet other foragers along the path.

Pickerelweed (Pontederia cordata): This is an aquatic plant found in ponds and still water edges. It is found throughout the East but has been tracked in the West to Oregon, where it is considered a noxious weed. In other states it is considered everything from a nuisance to threatened and in need of protection.

This tall plant grows nearly 4 feet tall. The leaves are shiny green and heart shaped. The flowers grow as spikes up to 4 inches long, deep blue to violet. The plant is very striking in bloom. As with the day lily, flowers bloom and last but one day. The tan, egg-shaped fruits have edible seeds inside.

Parts used: Young leaves, as salad or cooked greens. Seeds are full of starch and highly nutritious. They can be added to breakfast cereal or roasted and ground for flour.

Pigweed: See Amaranth, Lamb's Quarters and Purslane

Pine, Colorado Piñon (Pinnus edulis), Single-leaf Piñon (P. monophylla): In the Northwest we love our pines, firs and cedars. When visiting the desert lands we especially enjoy the Piñons. We also enjoy Piñon nuts. Unlike most evergreen trees, Piñons are created for the desert and are nearly as hardy and drought tolerant as cacti and other desert dwellers. They range throughout the Southwest but thrive better at elevations higher than 4,000 feet. Piñons are not big trees, rarely exceeding 40 feet. The leaves are straight and pokey, usually growing in groups of 2 or more.

Parts used: Nuts and seeds are edible, full of oil, packed with protein, the most flavorful pine nut to be had. They are extracted, although not easily, from the Piñon cone. Medicinally, the dried leaves

and the inner bark are used as a tea. The bark has much stronger properties. It is a diuretic and an expectorant. The resin or pitch from the tree is very sticky and abundant; you will have it on you before you know it. Natives used it to waterproof baskets and boats. Good for incense used as aroma therapy.

Plantain, Common (Plantago major) also Lance Plantain (P. lanceolata), Seaside Plantain (P. juncoides) and Wooly Plantian (P. media): This is not the starchy banana but a weed used as a green for salads and as a cooked green. Next to dandelion common plantain may be the most common naturalized weed in North America. It can be found in every state of the U.S. including Hawaii and Alaska and in most of Canada. Common plantain is common looking as well. The small plant grows usually no taller than 12 to 18 inches. It has broad oval leaves and spiky green to brown flowers. It has been used for millenniums as a pot herb and as a medicinal.

Parts used: As a food source the whole plant is gathered when the leaves are very young. It can be added to salads or cooked like spinach. The seeds are used as a seasoning. Medicinally the juice from the plant has been used as an infusion to treat digestive issues, ulcers, bladder issues. Considered a diuretic. A decoction of the plant is used for a variety of skin issues. Chewing the root has been used to alleviate a toothache.

Maureen Rogers' Wild Plantain Cookies

2 cups whole wheat flour
¾ cup plantain seeds, dried or fresh
4 Tablespoons baking powder
2 Tablespoons molasses
½ cup carob-covered raisins

Mix all ingredients well in a large bowl. Add tepid water to slowly form a thick, clay-like paste. To form cookies, roll a pinch of dough between your palms and press onto a greased cookie sheet. Bake 15 minutes at 350°F or until golden brown.

Prickly Lettuce: see Wild lettuce

Prickly Pear Cactus: See Cactus

Purslane, Common (Portulaca oleracea) aka Pigweed or Hogweed: Considered a naturalized weed or perhaps a native but one that was evident to North America before Columbus. Common purslane grows pretty much everywhere and in some places is considered invasive. Look for low lying smooth pink to red stems with alternate light green leaves that might remind you of the business end of an oar. The plant can flower year round depending upon habitat and moisture. The small five petal yellow bloom opens in the morning hours if the sun has been out.

Parts used: Leaves, as a salad green. Somewhat bitter and salty to the taste but still quite desirable. Stems, leaves and flowers are cooked quickly as you would spinach. The black seeds have been ground and used to make flour. Purslane is high in Omega-3 fatty acids plus Vitamins A, B and C. Medicinally, purslane has been used to treat slow digestive systems and urinary issues.

Redwood (Sequoia sempervirens): Wow, is there anything more impressive than a California redwood tree?! This species is found just along the Central and Northern

California coast plus a small stand near Brookings, Oregon. To walk in a grove of these ancient beauties is truly awe inspiring. It feels a bit like being in a sacred chapel in that you feel the need to be quiet and respectful. Redwood trees grow to heights of 300 feet and live 1,000 years or more. The thick bark is rusty red; the leaves are dark green and aromatic.

Parts used: Leaves and branches, gathered in the spring, are dried to make a tea which is good for colds and congestion.

Sagebrush, Big (Artemisia tridentate) Mountain Sagebrush (Artemisia vaseyana): This stuff is plentiful where I live. Its pungent aroma is a reminder that it is king of the flora in high desert lands. Big sagebrush is not related at all to garden sage and other salvia plants. It is actually related to mugwort, wormwood and tarragon. The name artemisia comes from the Greek fertility goddess, Artemis, or as the Romans called her, Diana.

My goats will eat sagebrush; but they'll eat pretty much anything. They enjoyed clearing a field for me to turn into pasture. Other livestock eat it only at last resort, and it's not liked by deer or pronghorn. It isn't very good for consuming by humans either. However, the natives used it for millenniums, making teas to help with a number of disorders. Sagebrush often grows to 6 feet tall, has grayish green leaves and woody branches. In spring, the small yellow flowers attract bees.

Parts used: The natives would take the leaves, dry and pulverize them into powder, then use it the way we use talcum powder. This powder is used topically as a first aid for skin wounds and as a disinfectant. Some people—not I—use a little as a seasoning or a tea.

Along the Path

One of my favorite books in the Bible is Paul's letter to the Ephesians. The first half of this letter is really a pep talk from God, through Paul, to a small band of Christians living in a city ruled by the occult. Ephesus housed one of the Seven Wonders of the Ancient World, the statue of Artemis (or Diana, as the Romans named her). You might picture in your mind a marble statue of a beautiful woman. That was not the case. The statue was garish, if not grotesque, in appearance. Artemis was considered the fertility god and was worshipped in strange and despicable ways, even including something as hard to imagine as temple prostitution.

The city and its inhabitants made their lucrative living from the temple and the many pilgrims that would come to worship there. The little band of believers that lived in the large city was a minority group who had truly set off on a different path than the rest of the population. From a temporal viewpoint it would have meant great financial loss and being ostracized by the rest of the town folk.

We, as people of faith, may feel put at a distance by those around us. We are called to be in the world and yet not of the world, ambassadors of the kingdom of Heaven. We are to plant seeds that may change the hearts of others. But it isn't hard to imagine that it may seem impossible, while nearly everyone else is living by and gaining from something you have chosen to reject.

We are to be mindful that our citizenship is not here and that we wait and work for something much better. Paul encourages us this way: "Praise be to the God and Father of our Lord Jesus Christ, who has blessed us in the heavenly realms with every spiritual blessing in Christ." (Ephesians 1:3)

While it may look like we have little, truly we "have it all" and we must keep our eyes on the prize.

Saguaro: See Cactus

St-John's-Wort, Common (Hypericum perforatum) aka Klamath Weed: In recent years no herb has garnered more interest and debate than this one. There are numerous varieties of this plant. Just in my area there are three: bog St-John's-wort, considered a native; common St-John's-wort, considered a noxious non-native; and western St-John's-wort, another native. Well over 300 of the species exist worldwide. Common St-John's-wort has been the herb of great interest for treating depression, seasonal adjustment disorder and other mood issues. The plant remains steeped in controversy regarding just how well it actually performs as an herbal. It is also unpopular with those who raise field crops and animals because of the adverse effect it can have on that industry. Common St-John's-wort is a transplant from Europe that now grows in much of the U.S. It is a beautiful, exotic-looking plant with shiny green leaves and bright 5-petal yellow flowers with multiple stamens.

Parts used: Flowers and leaves of the common St-John's-wort gathered fresh and made into tinctures, decoctions, and teas. Karen Mallinger (see page 119) uses St-John's-wort for its anti-inflammatory properties, in salves and liniments for sore muscles and even for burns.

Along the Path

When I first discovered St John's wort I was intrigued by the name. First I was curious about the word *wort*. Basically it is Old German for *plant*. But what about the St John part of the name? My first thought was that it had to do with St John the beloved disciple. But it wasn't *that* St John. It was John the Baptist. As best I can understand it, the name for the plant comes from a secretion of the leaves when you crush them in your hands. They exude a red-tinged liquid. Whoever came up with the name was well acquainted with the Bible to know that John the Baptist died a martyr's death— beheaded for his faithfulness to God.

John knew he was called to be the forerunner of Jesus, to proclaim that the Day of the Lord had finally arrived. Did he know where that journey would lead him— ultimately to his violent death? It's doubtful; none of us knows the final chapter of our life here on earth. We do, however, know the final outcome, if we faithfully serve. When we arrive on "the other side," we will hear from our Savior, "Well done, good and faithful servant."

I never want to walk by a St John's wort flower and be remiss in giving praise to God not only for what He created but for the spiritual lessons that are offered from the herbs. Perhaps considering St John's wort can strengthen us in our willingness and resolve to proceed on the narrow path of God, even though we cannot see around every bend ahead. As with willingness and faithfulness we take this journey of following unseen God on a narrow, winding path, we look forward to hearing, "Well done, good and faithful servant." (See Matthew 25:21.)

Salal or **Wintergreen**, Oregon Wintergreen (Gaultheria shallon, Gaultheria humifusa) Wintergreen, Checkerberry (Gaultheria procumbens, Western Wintergreen (Gaultheria ovatifolia): A gorgeous plant that grows to 4 feet and gets the name wintergreen from the brilliant green, shiny, oval leaves that really show off in the winter months when most all else has faded to gray and brown. In the West it is known as salal or Oregon wintergreen. The glossy leaves are thick and leathery. In spring beautiful urn-shaped, white to pinkish flowers hang in clusters. Come summer, berries develop in colors of dark blue to purple. The fruit is

Wintergreen

mealy, but the taste is exotic, like nothing else I have ever tasted. Salal grows on the west side of the Cascades and Sierras. It can be found along the Central California coast, and extending north all the way into Alaska. We found a cluster of berries, that wildlife hadn't yet plundered, while walking in the redwoods near the Smith River in Northern California. Along the Eastern Seaboard running from Canada to Alabama and Georgia it is known as wintergreen. Western wintergreen can be found in the Rockies, Yellowstone, and the Grand Tetons. The fruit of the wintergreen is redder in color. The plants usually grow in thickets.

Parts used: The leaves make a great tea. Wintergreen has long been used in similar fashion to mint. The berries are a food source but also medicinal. The leaves and berries are high in flavonoids, tannic acid and methyl salicylate. The plant has a number of medicinal qualities, from soothing sore throats to alleviating pain of sore muscles, sciatica and achy joints. Considered a good tonic for the circulatory system, a diuretic, helpful with the urinary tract and digestive issues. Topically, the leaves can be pounded into a poultice and used for skin complaints.

Salsify: Oyster Plant or Purple Salsify (Tragopogon porrifolius), Goat's Beard or Yellow Salsify (T. pratensis): These plants are identified by their striking colors and long, speared flower petals. Purple salsify grows across the country but prefers moist areas. Yellow salsify looks very similar in appearance to purple salsify but has a much broader range and can be found most places in the U.S. Both varieties are considered non-native, European transplants. They grow as biennials, to heights of 30 inches on single erect branches. The plants produce sticky latex which you can feel on your hands when you grasp the plant. The flowers will open and close depending on amount of sunlight.

Parts used: The whole plant. The roots and young shoots are used as a vegetable, which is said to taste much like oysters. Medicinally, the plant is an overall digestive aid.

Sassafras (Sassafras albidum) Part of the Lauraceae family, which includes California bay. This is an upright standing tree, with reddish brown, rough bark, growing to heights of 70-80 feet. It has barely-noticeable yellow flowers in the spring, and then oval, dark blue berries. The leaves are bright green and elliptical in shape, 3-9 inches long. These turn an array of colors in the fall. What also makes this tree unique is that you can get three shapes of leaves on the same tree; single oval leaves, 3-lobed leaves and on occasion, 5-lobed. It grows in much of the Northeast into the Midwest and also Texas, in damp woodlands and thickets. The leaves draw foragers because of their fragrance. When crushed they may remind you of citrus and vanilla. The twigs and bark emit a similar aroma. Sassafras has long been used for making bottled beverages, such as root beer.

Parts used: The root, fresh or dried. The leaves and bark for tea. The leaves can be dried, which enhances their flavor, and then crushed into a powder for various uses. Sassafras has a diuretic effect. It can help in the treatment of the symptoms of rheumatism. Topically it can be used to treat numerous skin disorders. In olden days, sassafras tea was considered a spring tonic to lift your spirits and ready you for the work of spring.

Caution: There has been some concern that sassafras contains a chemical that could cause liver damage and cancer.

Sea Grape (Coccoloba uvifera): You will have to travel to the warmest coastal areas in Florida to take advantage of this unique fruit. Sea grape grows as a large bush or small tree in many coastal areas there, right up to the sea. It is a beautiful evergreen tree with large, round leatherlike leaves. Note the red vein that runs up the middle of the leaf. Come spring the tree produces large grape-looking clusters of fruit that turn purple when ripe.

Parts used: The fruit is edible, delicious but tart. There is also a large pit to contend with. It is used by Florida folks to make jelly, jam, and even wine.

Serviceberry: See Juneberry

Shepherd's Purse (Capsella bursa-pastoris): Naturalized. Grows pretty much everywhere, especially near coastal or damp areas. Certainly found in suburban backyards. The lance-shaped leaves are reminiscent of dandelion and are consumed in much the same way. A member of the mustard family. The flower, blooming from early spring until winter's arrival, is small, white, with 4 petals on long stems. Plant grows from 6 to 20 inches.

Parts used: Leaves, before the flower buds, as salad or a cooked green. The dried seed pods are used in the same way as peppergrass, dried and ground. Medicinally, the whole plant is used for an infusion, decoction or tincture, for numerous complaints. Shepherd's purse has astringent and diuretic qualities. It is considered a tonic for kidneys and for an inflamed urinary system. It has been an effective medicine to stem hemorrhages, both internal and external, and used in difficult childbirths by knowledgeable midwives.

Sorrel, Common or Garden aka Spinach Dock or Narrow-leaved Dock (Rumex acetosa): Not related to wood sorrel. Common sorrel grows as a perennial and is a garden green for salads. In the wild you will not find it easily; but it is present here and there through much of North America. Non-native, naturalized from Europe. Look for alternate, oblong to oval, pale green leaves, somewhat reminiscent of dandelion leaves. The flowers are small nondescript white to green or white to red in color. When fully developed and in flower the plant can grow to 3 feet.

Parts used: The whole plant. Medicinally, the root is used as a diuretic, a laxative, and for troublesome menstrual cycles. The leaves are eaten like spinach. They are tart because of ascorbic acid contained in the plant; this is a caution for arthritis or rheumatism sufferers.

Spruce (Picea species) Brewer's Spruce (P. breweriana) Sitka Spruce (P. sitchensis) Black Spruce (P. mariana) Colorado Blue Spruce (P. pungens) Englemen Spruce (P. engelmannii) Red Spruce (P. rubens): I decided to include this wonderful tree for a couple of reasons. First, spruce trees grow nearly everywhere. Second, there is some intriguing research being done on the benefits of spruce. Over 30 varieties grow worldwide. Spruce trees grow as large evergreens with 4-sided sharp needles rather than leaves. The needles grow singularly from the branch. The trees produce cones. Spruce trees can live for a very long time. Some researchers have found Norway spruce trees that may date into the thousands of years, living potentially since the days of Noah's flood! Long used for lumber and paper production. The young shoots, inner bark and needles are considered edible.

Parts used: Needles, bark, essential oil and extract. The needle tips are used to make a wonderful concoction known as spruce tip syrup. You can nibble spruce leaves or make a tea. They are full of Vitamin C. The tea has been used to treat colds and flu. The cambium, or soft spongy inner bark, can be ground into flour. If you're out on the trail and forgot the chewing gum, try a little spruce pitch. Topically, spruce needles in a bath are said to be very soothing. Much research is being done on the extracted oil of the spruce tree. The extract contains a lignan which may be a cancer fighter and very effective in the treatment of prostate and breast cancer. It also seems to be helpful for menopause relief, cardiovascular health, and sexual function.

Colorado Blue Spruce

Sunflower, Common (Helianthus annuus): The wild sunflower has typical yellow petals and brownish/black center. By mid summer you can spot sunflowers along most sunny roadsides and fields. Birds and small animals rely heavily on these plants for food, and they are willing to work very hard to extract the many seeds from the flower head.

Parts used: Seeds, as good as the commercially-grown kind, but much smaller, requiring more work to extract. A great-tasting, nutritious food. Shelled seeds can be ground into a paste similar to peanut butter.

Harvest wild sunflowers when the flower heads droop and the leaves begin to die off. Dry in a warm, dry place out of direct sunlight. The sticky, sweet flower heads attract insects, especially ants, so watch for them. Dry them until easier to handle, then extract seeds using a rubber mallet to break them from the flower. This is not particularly easy, but once that is done, you just need to break open the shells. This is something to do during a really boring television program (I could name a few, if you would like). You can also pound the shells lightly, using the same rubber mallet, so as to get the job done faster.

Jerusalem artichoke (Helianthus tuberosus), a big rangy plant, is a wild cousin of the common sunflower. As a native plant it is found throughout the East and the Midwest. This is also a garden favorite because of its outstanding food value.

Parts used: The root or tuber, gathered in late summer. Tubers grow to the size of small sweet potatoes. They are cooked the same as potatoes but for a shorter time. The artichoke part of the name comes from the taste, similar to that of an artichoke heart. The tubers are high in potassium, niacin, iron, thiamine, and fiber.

Jerusalem Artichoke flowers and tubers

103

Along the Path

One year a sunflower sprouted in a place I had not planted one. Conditions were optimal and the plant grew to over 8 feet tall—too tall for me to see the giant flower. So I concentrated on the leaves, which are shaped like Valentine hearts. From the stem a single vein separates into three. This struck me as a perfect physical parable of something unseen: a picture of the Godhead, one in three and yet three in one. Father, Son and Holy Spirit are in concert with each other and yet separate in ministry and task.

I then noticed how the edge of the leaf is sharply serrated like a saw blade that would cut you if you were to rub your hand against it. This I pondered also. I could see an expression of godly love in the shape of the leaf and the picture of the triune being and purpose of God in the three connected veins. Now it occurred to me that God's love for us was so severe that it drew willing blood. "Yet we consider him stricken by God, smitten by him, and afflicted. But he was pierced for our transgressions . . . and by his wounds we are healed" (Isaiah 53:4-5). The Son bled and died for those he created.

My picture was now complete, but the lesson was not over.

This year I watched the sunflowers bloom. First the flower head emerges from the stalk. It is all tightly wrapped in outer leaves so you can't really tell what is going on until one day there is the bright, yellow-rayed flower, shining like the sun. This Bible verse came to mind: "The Son is the radiance of God's glory . . ." (Hebrews 1:3).

We may see the handiwork of the invisible Creator, Father God, and learn much about him from what we see; but it is through Jesus Christ, as revealed in his life and chronicled in the Bible, that we truly get our glimpse of God. Jesus shines with the glory of the invisible God and he is "the exact representation of his being." If you want to see God, then you must look at Jesus. He is the exactness of God because he is God.

Sweet Gale or Bog Myrtle (Myrica gale): This is a deciduous, low-lying shrub, strongly aromatic and reminiscent of sage. It has greenish gray, serrated oval leaves. The plant produces unique fruit that looks like little pine cones. Sweet gale is found in riparian areas and is native to the great Northeast, Southeast, and into the Midwest. This is a tea plant.

Parts used: The leaves, dried for a tea; leaves and nuts, dried for use as a spice or seasoning as you would sage. The leaves have long been used as an insect repellant.

Tumbleweed (Salsola tragus) aka Russian Thistle: What comes to mind when you think of the tumbleweed? For us lovers of the Old West, it is as intrinsic as six guns, Stetson hats, horses, cattle drives, ghost towns, Boot Hill and the Sons of the Pioneers. Like most of those things, tumbleweed is an immigrant to the U.S.

It is believed some of the seeds of this plant were shipped to America with flax seeds. This is actually one of a number of species of the salsola or thistle family that made their way to the states. This plant grows as an annual throughout much of the U.S. In the fall it dries up and detaches itself from the root and the ground. In spring the plant is green, red or purple and thorny with many stems and indistinct flowers. From the flower grow seed capsules. Tumbling in the wind is how this plant reproduces.

Considered a noxious plant, it consumes water and chokes out essential plants and crops. Often associated with erosion and drought. Not much good news; but it's edible.

Parts used: Early on, after the plant's appearance in the 1870s, natives began to consume it. Before they get too thorny the young plants can be picked. Don Wells, a wild plant enthusiast, says that you can take the young plant, wash it in a little salted water, then put a small amount of the plant with some fresh water in a microwavable bowl and cook on high for no more than 45 seconds. Then plunge it immediately into ice water. Consume as a green or toss in a salad. You may enjoy the flavor and get rid of a few weeds, too.

Young Tumbleweed

Uva Ursi: See Bearberry

Walnut (Juglans nigra): See Butternut

Watercress (Nasturtium officinale & N. microphllum formally Rorippa nasturtium-aquaticum): Whew, that is a lot of Latin for a pretty but common plant. Watercress is a non-native plant, found pretty much everywhere in or near water—ponds, eddies in streams, and ditches. In some places it is considered invasive and noxious. Sprawling rootstalks send up hollow stems and compound leaves with oval leaflets. Easily identified by small white or green flower clusters. Often found growing in huge mats on still water.

Parts used: The whole plant, but specifically the leaves before the flower blooms. Great as a salad green or cooked as a pot herb, or extracted for its juice. It has been consumed for millenniums. It is raised commercially and if you are a fan of V8 juice then you are drinking watercress. It is related to mustard and has a similar peppery taste. As an herbal, watercress has significant amounts of calcium, iron, folic acid, Vitamins A and C. It is full of antioxidants, is a digestive aid, and a diuretic.

Warning: It is very important to pick watercress from a water source that has not been polluted or come in contact with herd animals such as cattle. Also, watercress can sometimes be confused with water hemlock. Finally, it is a strong herb and should be used medicinally only with qualified guidance.

A vole hiding in Watercress

Wild Basil (Satureja vulgaris): I love living in the West, but this wonderful little plant could make me consider moving east. If you are a pesto fan, then you love your basil. Wild basil can be found along the Eastern Seaboard, in many places, from fields to forest edges, along roadsides, and to the seashore from up into Canada into the South. It has reportedly been found in the Pacific Northwest, in the Southwest, in the Rocky Mountains states, and in the Midwest. Considered a native plant and not a garden escapee. The plant can grow up to 1½ feet tall. The appearance is that of your common garden basil, dark green with downy leaves. The flowers are pink to purple.

Parts used: Specifically the leaves, but the stems as well. You can make a tea and enjoy its subtle taste, which is milder than our garden and commercially-grown varieties. Medicinally, basil may chase off a headache. This lovely plant is also a diuretic. Use wild basil for same culinary purposes as the basil you grow in the garden. To come across this plant is to find a great treasure, I think.

Wild Carrot or **Queen Anne's Lace** (Daucus carota): A pretty flower, very noticeable in the heat of the summer, often when everything else has faded away. It grows as a biennial, reseeding itself for new plants after the second year. We have lived in places where wild carrot is so profuse that it covers whole fields. A naturalized plant that is in some places considered noxious and invasive.

Before the plant flowers you probably wouldn't even notice it unless specifically looking for it. The immature stem looks like your garden variety carrot. Our domestic carrot is indeed a cultivar of Queen Anne's lace.

The flower, growing to 2 feet, is aptly described by its name. White, lacy umbels often have lavender-colored flowers in the center. The plant smells like a carrot, when pulled, which is important to note because this is another plant that looks similar to poison hemlock. Unlike poison hemlock, though, the stems and leaves are covered in fine hairs. As the flower ages it fades from striking white to a bird's-nest look.

Parts used: The roots in the first year, early in the season, eaten just like garden carrots. They're best cooked. Wild carrot is similar in properties to garden carrot. It acts as a diuretic, is helpful for the eyes, and is a digestive aid. A wild carrot soup is said to help relieve a number of digestive complaints.

Wild Mustards (Brassica species & Sinapsis species), Black Mustard (B. nigra), Field Mustard (B. rapa) White Mustard (S. hirta): A number of types and varieties of plants are known as wild mustard. Most, if not all, are naturalized to North America. More than likely some variety of mustard grows in or near your area. There are also a number of similar looking plants that are considered mustards, but are not. On long hairy stems, with multiple branches towards the top, it is the small yellow 4-petal flowers, growing in abundance, that give the plant distinction. As the plant grows, seed pods develop.

Parts used: The young leaves, unopened flower buds, the green seed pods, and the mature seeds. They will have the distinct smell and taste of mustard. Wild mustards are highly nutritious, full of vitamins and proteins.

Along the Path

For years I have written about Jesus' parable of the mustard seed and faith. For me, my earliest memories of church come from a handmade card a Sunday school teacher gave me. Inside the card was taped a little mustard seed. It was also my first introduction to the concept of herbs and their spiritual impact.

"As small as a mustard seed"—First we need to believe that there is a God and that the Bible is the book about God and that Jesus Christ is God who is our savior. This believing is our human part, made possible by God's prevenient grace, and because we are made in the image of God. Then, when we choose to believe, God's great gift comes to us. He deposits saving and achieving faith into our hearts and lives through his Holy Spirit. Like the mustard seed, our human belief can grow a hundredfold into believing faith. Human belief can be halting, faint and false. Faith from God is strong, steady and secure. As humans we cry out, "I believe, help me overcome my unbelief" (Mark 9:24). True faith, a gift from God, turns our halting beliefs—and our unbelief—into surety, regardless of what life throws at us.

Wild Oregon Grape (Mahonia aquifolia) aka Barberry and Mountain Holly. Appearance is similar to holly, with shiny, dark green serrated leaves. As an Oregonian I can say this is certainly one of my favorite plants, but it is found in many other places as well. A number of varieties exist. Named for the appearance of the fruit, it is really a berry. It is found in most places of the West. Much denser on the west side of the Cascades; but I have seen large expanses of the plant on the east side, usually close to water.

Parts used: Berries and roots. Fruit is edible when ripe, when the berry turns dark blue and malleable. Berries and root are used for a tea or decoction, as a blood tonic or purifier. It has diuretic qualities; is used as a tonic for the spleen and liver. A tincture may help skin conditions such as acne, eczema, and psoriasis.

Jams and jellies are made, usually requiring a one-to-one ratio of sweetener to fruit. We use honey, agave nectar, Stevia or sugar. Enjoy the unique taste and benefit.

Wild Parsnip: See Cowparsnip

Wild Plum (Prunus Americana) Canada or Black Plum (P. nigra) Beach Plum (P. marintima): Wild Plum, an American original, can be found growing as a native in most states except Texas, most West Coast states, Alaska and Hawaii. Canada plum ranges mostly in Canada but can also be found in some of New England and the Midwest. We have come across wild plum trees in places we didn't expect and can only assume that it was naturalized. Beach plum is found along the New England coast and down to Delaware. The trees grow to heights of 25 feet, but more likely you will find them growing as shrubs in thickets. Oval leaves; white to pink flowers in spring. Wild plum is yellow to red, Canada plum is orange to red.

Wild Plums, still green

Wild plum has been used as the cultivar for many of our plum trees. The fruit is half the size of commercially grown plums. In many places of the U.S. you can find these fruits growing in abundance. Some varieties have a blunt thorn that may surprise you.

Parts used: The fruit is eaten like commercial plums, but more likely cooked for jams or jellies. As an herbal, it has a laxative effect. The inner bark, once utilized by the natives for a tea, was said to help with irritations of the mouth and throat.

Wild Pacific Plum (Prunus subcordata): A wondrous little fruit that is related to and often confused with wild cherry. Wild Pacific plum grows in isolated areas east of the Oregon Coast Range but in more abundance in the Great Basin lands of the high desert areas of Southern Oregon, Northern

California, and Western Nevada. It also grows at elevations of 4,000 to 7,000 feet. A small tree or large bush, it grows in thickets any place where the roots can run deep to get water. Leaves are small, green and oval-shaped. Often, as summer advances, these leaves are the first to be touched by fall, even as early as mid-August. In fact, that is what we look for to identify where the trees are and know that fruit is ready for picking.

Wild Oregon Plum Tree

Parts used: Fruit. Wild Pacific plum has one of the highest carbohydrate content of any fruit, giving it a high food value and making it a plus for the animals that eat it. About the size and appearance of red cherries; the taste, though quite tart, is more like plum. Makes great jam, jelly or syrup. Cook thoroughly; add equal amounts of pectin and sweeteners.

Wild Rose (Rosa species): Numerous varieties grow across the U.S. Wild rose tends to grow much smaller and less developed than many of our garden and hybrid varieties. But the healthful benefits pack a large punch. The bushes have thorns aplenty and 5- to 7-petal flowers. Flower colors are light to dark pink.

Parts used: The petals can be eaten. They can be tossed with a salad or used to make fine-colored and tasty jellies or confections. The hips offer the true food and medicinal value. These develop after the flower withers away. Rose hips are one of the best sources of Vitamin C. They may have as much as 33 times more Vitamin C than the average orange. Rose hips are gathered in late summer to early fall. Animals like them too. Eat them right off the branch for a puckery snack. The seeds make them mealy. The best use is to make tea. Steep in near-boiling water for 10 minutes. Can also be cooked and processed for jams, jellies and marmalade. Many foragers use rose hips and make their recipes available online.

Wild Strawberry (Fragaria): A rare treat. The plant is plentiful; the fruit is rare. Perhaps not so rare to all of the animals that get to them first. For we humans to find a few is pretty hard. The wild strawberry plant, flower and berry are like a miniature version of what we cultivate. Wild strawberries grow in a wide range, from varieties along the West Coast, up into the damp areas of the mountains, and in the dry great basin. They can be found on the plains, along all sorts of waterways on the East Coast, inland to the Rockies, and up to sub-alpine elevations. A ripe berry is a sweet find with an incredible burst of flavor.

Parts used: Upon sampling them, I could not believe that so much flavor could be packed into such a small morsel. You can also utilize the leaves for teas; they are as full of vitamin C as the fruit. The fruit and leaves have a cleansing effect and are mildly diuretic; also a digestive aid. Acting as an astringent, the leaves are used topically for eyewash, and even for treating constipation with an enema.

Willow (Salix Species) Many varieties, including Black Willow, Grey Willow, Arctic, Whiplash, Pussywillow and Godding Willow: Probably no plant is easier to locate than this one. You may not even need to leave your yard. There are over 300 species growing from tiny plants to great trees that reach up to 100 feet, and in many shapes. For the most part, these hardy trees grow abundantly near good sources of water.

Parts used: Root, bark, and leaves: The bark and leaves are steeped into a tea and used as an astringent topically and as a digestive aid, a heart tonic, and a calmative. The bark can be soaked in cold water, pounded and gently boiled into a poultice to help

with skin issues. Perhaps its greatest use is as a pain killer, with its substantial levels of Salicin. This substance is closely related to aspirin. Natives learned, when they were plagued with headaches, arthritis and other complaints, that chewing the bark helped relieve the pain.

Along the Path

In Northern European countries some people had customs of using willow branches to celebrate Palm Sunday because of the unavailability of palm branches. In the Bible, willow is mentioned numerous times—usually, though, in connection with sorrow and times when Israel was held in captivity.

In Psalm 137:1-2, the psalmist says, "By the rivers of Babylon we sat and wept when we remembered Zion. There on the poplars (or willows, depending on translation) we hung our harps." They used the trees to hang up their musical instruments of joy and praise. In captivity it was too hard to play and praise. It is possible that the weeping willow was named, not just for its appearance, but because people would sit under it and mourn. It is interesting that the scientific name for that tree is Selix babyilonicia, thus stating a relationship to the very country that the people of Israel were carried off to after the reigns of David and Solomon. This happened because the nation had fallen away from God and fallen into sin. The word 'Babylon' is often related to sinful and despicable acts. The Bible states that Babylon has fallen, will fall again, and those caught up in their sins will fall too.

Witch Hazel, Common (Hamamelis virginia): This tree is native to the East Coast, from Maine to Florida, but may be found elsewhere in gardens, parks and arboretums. Common witch hazel grows as a small tree with an average height of 10 to 20 feet. The tree is deciduous with oval, rough-edged leaves that turn yellow in fall. The yellow flowers are unique, narrow and stringy. The flowers don't bloom until fall and so are on the

branches at the same time as the leaves and the leaf buds waiting for the next spring. In fact the common Latin name for the plant means "together" as leaf, flower and bud all grow at the same time. The intriguing common name has its ancestry in witchcraft, and in the fact that the branches were used as divining rods in locating water ("water witching").

Parts used: Bark, leaves, and seeds. I use witch hazel extract for my skin and hair, especially after shaving or for treating sweaty or inflamed armpits. The scent of witch hazel reminds me of the old barbershops where a man would splash on talcum and witch hazel after a shave and haircut. The extract, still widely available in stores, is also used for a number of skin complaints, such as insect bites and acne. It is also a safe and effective medicine for hemorrhoids. Tinctures are made by gathering the bark in the winter and soaking it in a mixture of ethyl and rubbing alcohol for two weeks. Though there is evidence of witch hazel being used internally, its best uses are external.

Wolfberry, aka **Pale Desert Thorn** (Lycium pallidum Miers; and also the rare variety Lycium oligosperma): The North American variety of one of the most touted of super foods or super fruits known as goji berry. These days the wolfberry is being exploited for its numerous benefits. When you see this listed in most products, it refers to wolfberry's Chinese cousin, goji. The plant's name comes from people's observation of wolves eating the berries. These canines are considered carnivores, so that is interesting.

The wolfberry that grows in North America has been discovered in California, Nevada, Utah, Arizona, New Mexico, Southern Colorado, Oklahoma and Texas, usually at elevations below 3,000 feet. They have been discovered in much higher elevations in such warm ranges as the Superstition Mountains in Central Arizona. We spotted some plants in Madera Canyon.

This thorny, shrubby plant grows to a few feet tall and is often found in loose thickets. Wherever you find one, you will usually find more. The leaves are pale green, oblong and elongated. In early spring greenish-cream colored

flowers appear, often tinged in violet. Small, red, oval fruit matures in late spring and throughout the summer. The berries contain many small seeds. If you hope to pick some, you need to be Johnny-on-the-spot, because birds and rodents prize them.

As mentioned, wolfberry benefits are highly regarded. The berries are loaded with Calcium, Potassium, Iron, Zinc, Selenium, Riboflavin or Vitamin B2, Vitamin C and such essential photochemicals as Beta-carotene and Zeaxanthin, plus Polysaccharides. And they taste very good. One expert in the field told me that the American variety is not as beneficially complete as the Chinese goji, but that is no reason not to enjoy it. Now people are consuming wolfberries with hopes of improving longevity, strengthening the immune system and muscles, increasing energy, and improving vision and eye health.

Parts used: The berries, best processed as jam, sauce, syrup, or juice. Medicinally, the leaves and roots have been used to treat skin wounds and toothaches. Some people drink a tea or infusion of the new green branches for a cold remedy.

Wood Sorrel (Oxalis species), Common Wood Sorrel (O. montana), Redwood Sorrel (O. oregana), Trillium-leaved Sorrel (O. trillifolia), Violet Wood Sorrel (O. violacea) Yellow Wood Sorrel (O. stricta) plus other varieties: This plant is not related to common sorrels. There are hundreds of varieties of this plant found in much of the U.S. and Canada, depending upon area and hardiness zone.

Grows as an annual reseeding itself yearly, or as a perennial in milder areas. The leaves will remind you of 3-leaf clovers or shamrocks, but are more delicate in appearance. You are more likely to find sorrel growing in a woodsy setting, appreciating the shade of the forest trees and shrubs. It can be found along riparian areas and prairie settings. When in flower, in spring, the petals are 5 in number and the color usually white; but depending on what the plant is feeding upon, you can get an array of colors. From the flower grows a small seed capsule containing a few seeds.

Wood Sorrel

Parts used: The leaves, which have a sour or tart taste, reminiscent of lemon. As an identifier, if it doesn't have a sour taste, then it may not be sorrel. The leaves, better in the spring and early summer, can be a nice trail nibble or gather enough to be added to salads. Excellent flavor as iced tea: steep leaves in warm water, as you would a sun tea. As a medicinal, the tea is used to treat digestive issues. As a topical, the leaves, again in the tea, help to treat skin irritations. Leaves are high in Vitamin C.

Caution: Because of the presence of oxalic acid, which is considered a toxin, too much use of sorrel leaves can slow down the absorption of calcium in the body.

Redwood Sorrel

Yarrow (Achillea millefolium): I grew yarrow long before I knew it was a beneficial herb. I liked its wild looks and long-lasting flowers. The cultivated varieties come in a number of colors. Wild yarrow flowers are usually only seen in white, sometimes with a hint of pink.

Yarrow has a long history and one of its names is soldier's wound wort. The erect plant can grow to 2 feet tall or more, with grayish-green leaves and umbel-type flowers. This hardy plant can exist in most climates and is native or naturalized in most parts of North America. Yarrow is steeped in history, folklore, and even the occult. Its scientific name, Achillea millefolium, is attributed to the Greek god, Achilles. Legend has soldiers of the Trojan War utilizing it to bind their wounds.

Parts used: The whole plant. Leaves are edible as a unique green, steamed like spinach or dried for seasoning. Medicinally, leaves used internally are considered anti-inflammatory because it is high in the chemical compound Azulene. Yarrow is utilized for colds and fevers because it causes one to perspire, helping to break a fever. It may also help normalize high blood pressure and help with indigestion. For a tea, steep in near-boiling water 10-15 minutes. Externally, it has been used for millenniums to treat wounds and nose bleeds.

Warnings: Large doses could increase the risk of headaches; external use can cause skin rashes. Yarrow can be confused with poisonous plants such as water hemlock.

Yerba Buena (Clinopodium or Satureja douglasii): I first found out about this plant while I was pastoring a little church in the foothills along the South Umpqua River in Southwest Oregon. Some of the old timers swore by this as the herb to take when the cold and flu season struck. They would use it topically, too, for an assortment of skin problems, such as rashes.

Yerba buena is a small perennial that grows as a twisting, trailing vine in the shady parts of a forest, intermixed with other plants. It is easy to miss; more than likely you will step on it before you notice it. But when you do, you may notice a wild minty aroma. The plant is found mostly along the California Coast and on the west side of the Cascades, but also in the mountains of Northeastern Washington and a short range into Canada. This vine will attach itself anywhere it can, in order to produce another plant. The leaves are bluish green, heart-shaped and serrated. The small flower is trumpet shaped and mostly white, sometimes tinged with a purplish hue.

Parts used: Stems, leaves, and flowers. The name loosely means "the good herb"; there are certainly some good attributes to this plant. Best used as a tea which is easy to make by taking the parts and steeping them in boiling water for 10 minutes. It makes a nice tea. And if you are suffering from a cold, flu, or similar complaint, you may notice that this good herb makes you feel better.

Yucca, Spanish Dagger (Yucca Arizonica), Banana Yucca (Y. baccata), Soaptree Yucca (Y. elata), Joshua Tree (Y. brevifolia): Yucca are hardy desert plants of which there are numerous varieties, including the majestic Joshua tree found in the Southern California and Nevada deserts. Yuccas are identifiable by the long dagger-like leaves that form in masses at the base of the plant. In the case of the Joshua tree, the leaves are at the end of each branch. The plant forms flowers. On a long stalk bunches of bell-shaped creamy white flowers form. Most of the plant species produce a fruit; some look like small bananas.

The whole plant has been used, and not just for food; the fibrous leaves are used for textiles and as building materials. There isn't much of a tougher item than a yucca leaf. And the dagger part of the tip will stop you in place while drawing a little blood as well.

Parts used: For food, the flowers and fruits, especially the fruit from the banana yucca, which are quite edible. They all seem to have a laxative quality, so a little goes a long way. As for other uses, the roots of the soaptree yucca can be pounded to produce a soapy substance appropriate for washing clothing, body, and hair.

Staying on the Path

Turn back, if you will, to the dedication page. Notice the two Bible verses I picked. Your first thought might be, "These don't really go together." One verse talks about the lover portrayed in the Song of Solomon gathering plants for his beloved. The next verse is attributed to Jesus Christ speaking of some fine day when he gathers us to himself to live with him forever, when all things become new.

I found a relationship between the two scriptures, and it came to me in an interesting way. A Christian friend of ours opened a preschool recently. She named it Heaven's Garden. If you knew her, you would understand. To me she is the epitome of who God would pick for a person to lead a children's ministry. She truly sees all the children as flowers in God's garden.

I suspect, in a similar way, God sees us that way too. If we are his, if we have given over our lives to him, accepted his freely-given sacrifice, seek to emulate Christ in our lives, then we are part of heaven's garden. In a sense we are transplants in this world, never to be naturalized in this present system. This is not our home. Like the lover in Song of Solomon gathering herbs for his beloved, Jesus will one day gather us to be part of his heavenly garden, his renewed creation, for all eternity.

Think a little more about the man and woman in Song of Solomon. Imagine the joy when the lover brought all those wonderful lilies back to his beloved. I am sure the sweet fragrance that filled the room was a heady reminder of the love between these two.

In the same way, think upon this: "For we are to God the aroma of Christ among those being saved and those who are perishing" (2 Cor. 2:15). The next verse states that we are to be the "fragrance of life." Blossom where you are, give off a sweet fragrance to all who are around you, and in due time God will gather you and take you home.

Friends on the Path

Wild herb foraging and use is happening all over the country. This interest has brought me in contact with a number of professional and amateur herbalists. Some of these friends and contacts have shared with me what wild herbs they find in their area and what they like to do with them. I'm passing on this information to you from Karen, Mike, Tina and Pamela in hopes these tips will be of help to you in your search for, and enjoyment of, God's wild herbs.

Karen Mallinger was born in England and raised in the Amish country of Northern Ohio. She grew up with a natural love of the earth and plants. Gardening was a regular part of family life along with the *Old Farmers Almanac*, using its suggestions for garden and animal care.

As an adult she settled in Colorado and began growing organic vegetables and herbs. She also began an intensive program towards getting her degree as a Doctor of Naturopathy, focusing on women's health, geriatric health, and "wholistic" animal and pet care. She obtained her MH, CNC and CHS certifications from Trinity College and is a Certified Natural Health Professional. Her personal calling is to provide clients and customers with good things from the good earth. "I believe that God has provided everything we need for optimal health in the way of natural plants and herbs and seek to educate others on the path to natural health and total wellness."

Karen now resides in Michigan's beautiful Upper Peninsula with her husband, Michael and three Pembroke Welsh Corgis.

Karen owns and operates All Goode Gifts. She specializes in custom made herbal formulations and wellness teas for specific ailments or personal care issues. Karen speaks publicly and conducts workshops on the subject to various groups. She is a contributor of articles to *Essential Herbal Magazine*, *Herb Quarterly*, and other publications.

You can email her at allgoodegifts@yahoo.com or visit her online store at URL: http://www.allgoodegifts.com.

Karen indicates that she is "blessed with a plethora of wild herbs that are very useful for the issues we find most often here," in Michigan's upper peninsula. The growing season is short in the north country of the U.S. She lists her favorites as burdock, mullein, St John's wort, plantain and jewelweed.

In Karen's words:

"Burdock is a wonderful blood-cleansing herb that is prolific here. The root can be used in cooking, and I often harvest the young roots and grill them with some carrots, garlic and onions. In Japan it is a staple and known as Gobo. I also make a tincture with it that is very helpful for my clients with skin issues. I use burdock in many of my medicinal teas when blood cleansing and liver health are issues. It is a mild digestive stimulant and can be used in a tea to help with indigestion.

"Mullein is another herb that grows prolifically here. It is also known as 'girl scout's toilet paper.' I think this is probably due to the large fuzzy leaves, which are quite soft and would make a fitting substitute if needed. Please note that some people are irritated by the fine hairs, so be cautious if using in this manner.

"Mullein is a very hardy biennial that can sometimes get as tall as 6 feet. All parts of the plant are useful. Its primary properties are anodyne (pain reliever), antispasmodic (eases muscle cramps), demulcent (soothes irritated tissues), diuretic, expectorant, vulnerary (encourages wound healing), sedative, anti catarrhal (reduces mucous) emollient and pectoral. It is my 'go to' herb for any type of lung issues. I use it in tinctures and teas predominantly. I also make a wonderful, infused ear oil that contains mullein flowers and garlic infused in organic olive oil. You can also use the flowers to make a lovely pale-yellow dye.

"St John's wort is my favorite herb. It is so versatile and grows everywhere up here where winters are long and seasonal affective disorder (S.A.D.) is prevalent. This herb has traditionally been used for depression in Europe for many years. But many people don't know that it also has anti-inflammatory properties. For this reason, I use it in salves and liniments for athletes or for Dad after a long day of snow blowing!

"St John's wort makes a wonderful tea or tincture and can be used for burns. You'll know you have the right flower when you rub the pistils in our fingers and they leave a red stain. People up here often see the 'herb lady' walking along the roads with a gallon jug full of the brilliant yellow flowers. Be aware that St John's wort does contain photo-toxins, which may result in photosensitivity in fair skinned individuals when exposed to bright sunlight. Though there are no documented cases of this condition in people using the herb, the potential does exist and proper precautions should be taken.

"Plantain should look familiar to everyone; it is common all over the country. It is hemostatic (arrests bleeding and hemorrhaging), a decongestant, demulcent, and vulnerary. Because of this last attribute, it can be used in place of comfrey for treating bruises and broken bones. It can be used as a poultice for drawing out splinters or infections. Since it is also hemostatic, if you happen to cut yourself while gardening, grab a few leaves, chew them up and put them on the wound. It will stop the bleeding and start the healing process. Plantain is also great for bee stings. I use it in teas, tinctures and also in salves to help with wounds or burns.

"Jewelweed is commonly known as 'touch me not' because the seed capsules will burst open at the lightest touch. The juice from the stems is a common remedy for poison ivy. What's interesting about this herb is that it is often found growing in close proximity to the poison ivy. Isn't God wonderful!? I use it to make an ointment for any type of itch or sting, as well as burns, sprains or other skin conditions."

Mike Middleton lives in the Pacific Northwest, specifically in an area southwest of Olympia, Washington. This young man and his wife, Sharon, served as youth ministers for us for a number of years. He has lived throughout the United States and has traveled to Mexico, Canada and Europe with Youth with a Mission (YWAM). He is also a musician, and he home-schools his son Micah. He is the author of two books of poetry, *Sacred Journeys* and *Modern Musings*. Mike is an avid outdoorsman and forager. He has long studied, collected and sampled herbs and other wild edible plants and is very knowledgeable on the subject.

He describes the area where he lives as a transition zone between the damp Puget Sound area and the drier, warmer plains area. Because of the mild climate he indicates that there is much to forage. He has found over sixty plants within a two mile area that he has sampled and used.

He finds blueberries, serviceberries, blackberries and raspberries along roadsides and in fields. He has found pear and apple trees growing in the wild. In areas near water he has found an abundance of elderberries and red huckleberries. He likes to roast elderberries with a sweetener before using them.

Mike looks for red sumac in parks and old abandoned home sites. He picks the berries when ripe, bruises them and then soaks them along with a few leaves in the refrigerator in a gallon of water for a few days. He strains out the liquid which he says makes for a wonderful lemonade-like drink which also has a medicinal value of easing a sore throat.

To make a variety of herbal teas he gathers the leaves and blossoms of blueberry, raspberry, wild rose, yarrow, mint, chamomile, fireweed, plus red clover and white clover.

He also gathers holly leaves. These are boiled for a jasmine-flavored tea. He notes that the berries should be avoided because they are considered toxic. He tends to dry the leaves for tea rather than using them fresh. He dries them on cookie sheets in the sun for a day.

A number of the plants he finds are utilized as food and many are found along roadside areas, fields and vacant lots.

He finds an abundance of plantain, lamb's quarters, miner's lettuce, purslane, sheep sorrel, and wood sorrel. These he uses as fresh greens for salads and such. He also finds dandelion and stinging nettle, which he cooks.

He has found wild wheat, turnips, and blue camas. He stresses that it is just the bulb of the blue camas that is eaten and that it is important to be watchful for death camas.

Mike loves cattail and introduced that to us. He eats the pealed stalks, which he compares to cucumber. The nodules on the roots he describes as something like a perfect little potato. He likes to eat the tails while still green, like corn on the cob. The pollen he collects later and mixes at a 1 to 1 ratio with flour to make sweet breads.

Mike finds three kinds of wild nuts in his area. These are hazelnuts, walnuts and acorns from the oak trees. Hazelnuts are more likely to be found in forest areas. He finds walnuts in and around old farms and fields. Acorns are plentiful.

Mike suggestions a few medicinal herbs that are easy to find in the Pacific Northwest.

Evening primrose flowers and leaves, which are edible. He has found that the flower rubbed on the skin is effective for such complaints as eczema, heat rash, and even cradle cap (it helped his infant son). And Mike likes to use yarrow during the cold and flu season.

St John's wort is another plant that grows profusely in the wet areas of the Northwest. He makes a simple tea from it, using the stems, leaves and flowers. The plant is dried and infused, producing a very calming beverage.

Here is Mike's recipe or formula for what he calls "flu-buster tea." He combines the following dried herbs: yarrow, rosehips, chamomile, blackberry or rose leaves. Other ingredients that can be added are: blueberries and the leaves, clover flowers. He then takes a coffee filter, puts the ingredients inside and staples it closed. This is steeped in just-boiled water and left until the mass of the herbs is reduced by a third. He is pleased with the results for himself, his family and friends.

Mike finds several varieties of hawthorn in his area and finds most of them bland and mealy but on one tree the fruit has an apple flavor. Sounds good, but its location is just for him and the birds to know.

Finally he is a fan of mullein, which is fairly common in fields and roadsides. He uses the dried flower spikes to make a tea for asthma and bronchitis. He uses an infusion of the leaves to treat a number of skin complaints from scrapes to rashes and other irritations.

Tina Samms is the editor of *Essential Herbal Magazine* and a writer and publisher of many articles and books. Tina is immersed in anything to do with herbs and is also a true forager and wild crafter. She gives credit to her grandfather as the catalyst. Together they would go on many walks and find wild strawberries, angelica and sassafras. She loves to go out these days, well equipped with boots, enamel pail, gloves, snips, baggies, and a couple of field guides.

She has been very helpful in providing information for my herb books. A number of recipes contained here and in *God's Healing Herbs* come from her, and from her magazine contributors.

Tina lives in Pennsylvania on fifteen acres that include a tree farm, a natural woodland area, and a wetland area by a creek. She finds elderberry, pawpaw and serviceberries there. She has also foraged and transplanted Jerusalem artichoke to fill a large patch on her property.

By simply wandering about her place and nearby she finds burdock, thistle, chicory and dandelion. Chickweed and purslane are so common that they threaten to take over her lawn area. She indicates that there are wild vegetables to be found throughout the year where she lives in Pennsylvania. She suggests waiting until after the first freeze in fall before gathering the tubers of Jerusalem artichoke, because that improves the flavor.

She suggests a wild salad of the following plants: daylily buds, violet flowers and buds, rose petals, sheep sorrel, young dandelion leaves, garlic mustard greens, chickweed, lamb's quarters and wild mustard.

You can find *Essential Herbal* on line at www.essentialherbal.com or by snail mail contact her at *The Essential Herbal*, 1354 N. Strickler Road, Manheim PA 17545.

Pamela Torres and her husband live in Boone, North Carolina. Her daughters and five grandchildren live near by. Pam is an organic gardener and a business owner specializing in edible flowers. She loves learning more about herbs and facilitates locally-based ongoing herb classes. Pamela has foraged in many places, loves to roam the woods but prefers cow pastures. She states that she lives in dairy country, so there are lots of pastures to choose from. Here are some of her favorite herbs and edibles:

Lamb's quarters: She finds plenty of this, which she prepares like spinach. She notes that it is rich in vitamins, minerals and other nutrients. Because it is plentiful she gathers much. In its fresh state she uses it to make pesto. She freezes individual portions of the pesto for use in pizza and pasta entrees. The rest of this harvest she dehydrates and stores for the winter months. She uses it in soups and lasagna, and grinds it into flour for cookies, pancakes, etc.

Dandelion: In the spring and summer she uses the leaves in salads. In the fall she digs the root for medicinal uses and to cook in soups.

In those same cow pastures she finds burdock, thistle, bee balm, milkweed, shepherd's purse, boneset, elecampane and meadowsweet. These she uses for vinegars, tinctures and infusions.

As a true forager she has found chamomile and transplanted a few of these plants back in her garden. She has learned that chamomile likes compact soil so she stomps around the plant to set it well.

She believes there is still much to discover and is grateful that God has provided it all. You can contact Pamela Torres at pamelat49@hotmail.com. You can write to her at 412 Howards Creek Church Road, Boone N.C. 29607.

Photo Credits

Photos © Kit Ellingson: A Trail at Tablerock-1 p.16; Agave p.17; A Trail at Tablerock-2 p.19; Arrowhead p.20; Arrow Leaf Balsam Root p.21; American Mountain Ash p.78; Aspen in summer p.22; Barrel Cactus p.33; Bearberry or Kinnikinik p.25; Chamomile p.37; Cheeseweed p.37; Chicory p.41; Cholla p.33; Path in John Day Fossil Beds p.40; Daylily p.52; Red Currant bush p.50; Red Currant fruit p.50; White Clover p.43; Coltsfoot p.45; Red Columbine p.46; Chiltepin p.43; Creosote p.49; Elderberry in flower p.52; Elderberry in fruit p.54; False Solomon's Seal p.55; Fiddlehead Fern p.55; Fireweed p.56; Wild Grape p.59a; Beaked Hazelnut p.59; Hedgehog Cactus p.33; Shagbark Hickory tree p.62; Horseradish p.62; Horsetail p.63; Huckleberry p.27; Coastal Huckleberry p.27; Hackberry p.60; Ironwood with parrot p.64; Madrone p.71; Honey Mesquite p.72; Miner's Lettuce p.75; Mullein p.80; Oak tree p.83; Ocotillo and cardinal p.86; Ocotillo flowers p.86; Oregon Broad-Leaf Maple p.71; Oregon Myrtle p.23; Paloverde p.87; Passionflower p.87; Patagonia Path p.42; Path at Upper Klamath p.29; Pennyroyal p.76; Redwood trees p.94; Sagebrush p.95; Saguaro Cactus p.33; Scouring Rush p.61; Stinging Nettle in rocks p.82; Thistle and butterfly p.74; Sagebrush Path p.95; Wild Alpine Strawberry p.111; Wild Carrot p.107; Wild Pacific Plum p.110; Willows at Lake Selmac p.111; Wintergreen p.99; Witchhazel p.113; Yucca p.116; Photo of Author p.128; Path at Hell's Canyon p.6.

Photos © Larry and Catherine Lawton: A farm road in Colorado p.10; Wild Asparagus p.21; Aspen Trees in Fall p.22; Blueberries, Maine p.27; Bunchberries p.31; Cattails p.34; Red Clover p.43; Blue Colorado Columbine p.46; Cottonwood trees, CO p.47; Cowparsnip p.47; Dandelion p.51; False Solomon's Sea p.53; Gooseberry p.50; Wild Ground Cherry Plant p.59; Juniper with Berries p.66; Wild Oregon Grape p.109; Hawthorn Berries p.61; Serviceberry bush p.65; Milkweed p.75; Mustard Plants p.107; Pinyon Pine, p.92; Prickly Pear Cactus p.33; Rosehips, Maine Coast p.110; Redwood Sorrel, California p.114; Wood Sorrel, Connecticut p.114; Colorado Blue Spruce p.102; Wild Rose p.110; Sunflowers p.103; White Sweet Clover and Yellow Sweet Clover, p.44; Tumbleweed p.105; Yarrow, Humboldt Coast p.115; Yellow Pond Lily p.69; Man and child on wooded path p.73; Wooded path in Sonoma County p.24; Trail through trees by river p.55; Trail through a mountain meadow p.65; Trail in Redwoods, CA p.68; Path through mountain forest near a creek p.77; Trail through Oak and Madrone Chaparral, Sonoma County p.81; Footprints, Lost Coast p.85; Big Horn Sheep on mountain road p.91; Paths in Rocky Mountain National Park pp.98, 112, 117; Paths near Poudre River pp. 123,127

Photos © Mike Middleton: Fire Pin Cherry, Oregon p.38; Salmonberry, OR p.28; Thimbleberry, OR p.28

Photos © Tina Samms: Burdock, Pennsylvania p.31; Chickweed (with penny for size), PA p.39; Curly or Yellow Dock, PA p.49; Lamb's Quarters, PA p.68; Mulberry, PA p.79; Persimmon, PA p.90; Plantain, PA p.93; Plantain, PA p.93; Sassafras, PA p.100; Sweet Gale, PA p.105; Wild Garlic, PA p.18; Wild Ginger Flower, PA p.58

Photos from Can Stock Photos: Bay Laurel p.23; Calamus p.34; Celery or Smallage p.35; Comfrey p.46; Forest Cranberry p.48; Wild Garlic flowers p.18; Ripe Ground Cherries p.59; Jerusalem Artichoke tubers p.103; Jojoba p.64; Kelp, Seaweed p.84; Garden Lovage p.70; Young Milkthistle seen from above p.74; Stinging Nettle leaves p.82; Wild Onion flowers p.18; Pawpaw blooms on tree p.88; Pecans p.88; Wild Persimmon tree in Tenessee p.90; Wild Green Plums p. 109; Purslane p.94; Western Salsify p.99; Seagrape p.100; Young water vole in Cress along a stream p.106; Wild Peppermint p.76; Country Path p.104; Road along a Vineyard p.108; Nature Trail in Kansas p.36

Photos from USDA (http://plants.usda.gov): American Eelgrass p. 35 by William & Wilma Follette. USDA NRCS. 1992. Western wetland flora: Field office guide to plant species. West Region, Sacramento. Courtesy of USDA NRCS Wetland Science Institute; Laurel nuts & leaves p.23 by John D. Guthrie. Provided by National Agricultural Library. Originally from US Forest Service. United States, OR. 1924; Buffaloberry p.30 and Siberian Crabapple p.48 and Black Walnut p.31 by USDA-NRCS PLANTS Database / Herman, D.E., et al. 1996. North Dakota tree handbook. USDA NRCS ND State Soil Conservation Committee; NDSU Extension and Western Area Power Administration, Bismarck; Beargrass p.25 by Clarence A. Rechenthin @ USDA-NRCS PLANTS Database; Bedstraw p.26 and Butternut leaves p.31 and Lotus flower p.70 and American Lotus leaves and flower p.69 and Pickerelweed p.92 and Shepherd's Purse p.101 and Red Chokecherry p.38 and Prickly Lettuce p.69 by Robert H. Mohlenbrock @ USDA-NRCS PLANTS Database / USDA NRCS. 1995. Northeast wetland flora: Field office guide to plant species. Northeast National Technical Center, Chester; Bitter Cherry p.38 by Sheri Hagwood @ USDA-NRCS PLANTS Database; Black Chokecherry p.38 by USDA-NRCS PLANTS Database; Blue Flax p.56 and Common Sheep Sorrel p.101 by Sheri Hagwood @ USDA-NRCS PLANTS Database; Ground Nut p.60 and Redroot Amaranth p.20 by Robert H. Mohlenbrock @ USDA-NRCS PLANTS Database / USDA SCS. 1989. Midwest wetland flora: Field office illustrated guide to plant species. Midwest National Technical Center, Lincoln; Jerusalem Artichoke p. 103 by Jennifer Anderson. United States, IA, Scott Co., Davenport, Nahant Marsh. 2001; Western Labrador Tea p.68 by W. Carl Taylor @ USDA-NRCS PLANTS Database / USDA NRCS. 1992. Western wetland flora: Field office guide to plant species. West Region, Sacramento; Mormon Tea p.78 by USDA-NRCS PLANTS Database; Pawpaw leaves p.88 by Robert H. Mohlenbrock. USDA SCS. 1991. Southern wetland flora - Field office guide to plant species. South National Technical Center, Fort Worth. Courtesy of USDA NRCS Wetland Science Institute; Pennycress p.89 by A.H. Carhart @ USDA-NRCS PLANTS Database; Alkali Pepperweed p.89 Courtesy of USDI BLM. United States, UT, Garfield Co.. October 2003; Virginia Pepperweed p.89 by Robert H. Mohlenbrock @ USDA-NRCS PLANTS Database / USDA SCS. 1991. Southern wetland flora: Field office guide to plant species. South National Technical Center, Fort Worth; Wild Basil p.106 © Forest and Kim Starr

Photos from Wikimedia: Yerba Buena p.115 by Gordon Leppig & Andrea J. Pickart at http://www.fws.gov/humboldtbay/plantguide/genus-s.html as Satureja douglasii; New Jersey Tea p.83 by U.S. Fish and Wildlife Service; Wolfberry p.113 by David H. Kinder, U.S. Fish and Wildlife Service.

Selected Sources

Listed here are books, periodicals, and internet resources that have helped me in writing this book and which you may find helpful in learning more about God's wild herbs. This is not an exhaustive list. I am continually finding sources of reliable information and I encourage you do the same.

Connecticut Botanical Society website: http://www.ct-botanical-society.org

Domico, Terry. *Wild Harvest: Edible Plants of the Pacific Northwest.* Hancock House, 1979.

Duke, James A. Ph.D. *The Green Pharmacy.* Rodale Press Inc./St. Martin's Paperbacks, 1997.

Ellingson, Dennis. *God's Healing Herbs.* Cladach Publishing, 2006.

Garden Trees. DK Publishing, 1996.

Gibbons, Euell. *Stalking the Wild Asparagus.* David McKay Company, 1962.

The Herb Companion (March 2008 and Sept. 2009). Ogden Publications.

Herb Master: Complete CD-ROM Herbal Reference Library. ACR Int., 1999-2003.

Houdret, Jessica. *Practical Herb Garden.* Herms House, 1999-2003.

Kavanagh, James and Raymond Leung. *Edible Wild Plants: an Introduction to Familiar North American Species.* Waterford Press, 2000.

———. *Wildflowers of the Pacific Northwest.* Timber Press, 2006.

Moore, Michael. *Medicinal Plants of the Desert and Canyon West.* Museum of New Mexico Press, 1989.

———. *Medicinal Plants of the Pacific West.* Red Crane Books, 1993.

Peterson, Lee Allen. *Edible Wild Plants: Peterson Field Guide.* Houghton Mifflin, 1977.

The PLANTS Database (http://plants.usda.gov, 13 August 2010). USDA, NRCS. 2010. National Plant Data Center, Baton Rouge, LA 70874-4490 USA.

Samms, Tina. "Under the Sun: The First Five Years." *The Essential Herbal Magazine* (2008) The Sibling Group.

Shaw, Richard and Marion A. Shaw. *Plants of Yellowstone and Grand Teton National Parks, Revised.* Wheelwright Publishing, 2008.

Wells, Don and Jean Groen. *Foods of the Superstitions—Old and New.* Self-published, 2003.

Wild Foods for Every Table, complied by Tina Samms. The Sibling Group, 2006.

Yetman, David. *Fifty Common Edible and Useful Plants of the Southwest.* Western National Parks Association, 2009.

Acknowledgments

I want to express my deepest gratitude to those who helped make this book possible.

First, the Cladach publishing family, Cathy and Larry Lawton and their adult children, who are discovering and turning out wonderful books. They also patiently put up with the quirkiness of authors.

Next, I thank the professional and amateur herbalists across the country who contributed information and photos. Without them I don't think this project would have been possible, or at least completed, in one's lifetime.

Last, but certainly not least, I thank my wife, Kit. She did much of the photography which often meant getting into places that no sane person should go just to obtain the correct light, backdrop, etc. And she puts up with being married to a writer and a dreamer.

About the Author

Dennis Ellingson has served as a pastor and a professional counselor. He continues to minister through a number of venues. He is a speaker and presenter on the subjects of herbs, grandparenting, and the Old West.

He is married to Kit, a professional photographer. He is the father of two grown children: Todd, who is married to Lori, and Wendy, who is married to Rob. He is also a grandfather and finds this the most rewarding of his accomplishments and experiences.

The Ellingsons reside in Southern Oregon and are the owners of the "God's Healing Herbs" research-based herb gardens. He is also known as The Herb Guy on Facebook and contributes tips, thoughts and devotions there on a regular basis.

Dennis's other titles published by Cladach are *The Godly Grandparent* (with his wife, Kit) and *God's Healing Herbs*.

I ♥ FASHION HAIR!

All rights reserved. No part of this publication may be reproduced, stored in a retrieval system or transmited, in any form or by any means, electronic, mechanical, photocopying, recording or otherwise, without the prior permission from the owners of the copyright.

"Queda prohibida, salvo excepción prevista en la ley, cualquier forma de reproducción, distribución, comunicación pública y transformación de esta obra sin contar con la autorización de los titulares de propiedad intelectual. La infracción de los derechos mencionados puede ser constitutiva de delito contra la propiedad intelectual (Art. 270 y siguientes del Código Penal). El Centro Español de Derechos Reprográficos (CEDRO) vela por el respeto de los citados derechos".

I love Fashion Hair!
Copyright © 2008 Instituto Monsa de Ediciones

Editor
Josep Mª Minguet

Layout, design and text.
Maquetación, diseño y texto.
Eva Minguet Cámara
Equipo editorial Monsa

© INSTITUTO MONSA DE EDICIONES
Gravina, 43
08930 Sant Adrià de Besòs
Barcelona
España
Tlf. +34 93 381 00 50
Fax +34 93 381 00 93
www.monsa.com
monsa@monsa.com

ISBN 10 84-96823-73-3
ISBN 13 978-84-96823-73-0

I ♥ FASHION HAIR!

monsa

The latest trends in men's and women's hairstyles are influenced by the newest cultural movements and the new roles being played out in today's society.

The cult of caring for your look and standing out from the rest is now a constant feature found among the general public, and these days we can see trends to suit anyone's likings.

The hottest fashions demonstrate the broad evolution that hairstyles have experienced in the last few years, the fruit of hairstylists' experimentation. Not only have they attempted to lend the most personality as possible to their creations, but also adapt to the profound and constant changes occurring in society itself. We can see how the masculine figure has stepped into this innovative whirlwind, along with a yearning to tailor the new trends as much as possible in search of originality, thus making hairstyle one of the basic elements that has determined the era in which we live. This inventiveness and drive to be different has caused the creativity of hairstylists to develop at astonishing speed over the past few years, whether in step with or parallel to the evolution of society. As a result, a so-called global individualized "look" has arisen to the point where the way of styling one's hair reflects a philosophy of life, even determining manner of one's speech. In taking a look at the latest trends covering all types of hairstyles, we discover completely cutting-edge and modern looks, not to mention the daring and fun ones. By travelling to different cities home to the best stylists of the moment, we map a varied and contemporary route around the latest ideas from international style figures.

Highlighting the attractiveness and personality of the work we present in this book, we outline the steps which trends set in today's society, as the quality of the images shown and the beauty of the work itself make the volume a comprehensive and rather enjoyable work of reference.

Another of our intentions in publishing this book is to place hairstyle and its creative labour in its deserved spot atop the international scene; we include important stylists from various nationalities such as; Patrick Cameron, Essensuals Evolution, Toni & Guy, Petra Mechurova, Sanrizz, Alan D, Trevor Sorbie, Anne Veck, Cebado, Felicitas, Hob Salons, Gym Groming, etc.

We hope that all the work presented here can put the latest trends within the reach of stylists and image consultants all over the world, thus giving them the most globally complete information possible.

INTRO

Las nuevas tendencias en el peinado femenino y masculino están influenciadas por los nuevos movimientos culturales, y los nuevos roles en la sociedad actual.

El culto a cuidarse y a ser diferentes, es ya una constante entre la población y es ahora cuando encontramos tendencias para todos los gustos.

Las últimas modas demuestran la gran evolución que el peinado ha sufrido en los últimos años, fruto del estudio realizado por los estilistas que intentan no sólo personalizar al máximo sus creaciones, sino también adaptarlas a la profunda y constante evolución que se produce en la sociedad. Es por ello que la figura masculina entra dentro de esta vorágine innovadora junto al afán de personalizar al máximo las tendencias buscando esa originalidad que hace del peinado uno de los elementos básicos para determinar la época en que vivimos. Esa originalidad y esa búsqueda de ser diferentes hace que la creatividad de los estilistas se haya desarrollado en los últimos años a una velocidad de vértigo acorde o en paralelo a la evolución de la sociedad. Se produce de esta manera el llamado look global del individuo donde su forma de peinarse muestra una filosofía de vida llegando incluso a determinar hasta su forma de hablar.

Mostraremos las últimas tendencias, pasando por todos los estilos del peinado, encontrándonos con looks totalmente renovados y actuales, ideas arriesgadas y divertidas, realizando un viaje por diferentes ciudades donde se encuentran los mejores estilistas del momento, dando de esta manera un recorrido variado y actual con las últimas propuestas de estas grandes figuras del estilismo internacional.

Resaltar el atractivo y la personalidad es la finalidad de todos los trabajos que presentamos en este libro, siguiendo las tendencias que la sociedad actual marca, por lo que la calidad de las imágenes presentadas y la belleza de los trabajos hacen del mismo una obra de completa y agradable consulta.

También dentro de nuestras intenciones al publicar este libro es colocar al peinado y su labor creativa en su merecida proyección internacional, contando para ello con grandes estilistas de distintas nacionalidades; Patrick Cameron, Essensuals Evolution, Toni & Guy, Petra Mechurova, Sanrizz, Alan D, Trevor Sorbie, Anne Veck, Cebado, Felicitas, Hob Salons, Gym Groming, etc.

Esperamos que todos los trabajos aquí presentados pongan al alcance de estilistas y creadores de imagen las últimas tendencias realizadas en todo el mundo, dando de esta manera una información internacional lo más completa posible.

Petra Mechurová / collection Day After

Ishoka / collection Ishoka

Felicitas / collection Suit Bob

Kuhn the School / collection Stones

Mark Leeson / collection Hair, Body and Mind

Petra Mechurová / collection Essence

Mahogany / collection Art Cube-Esque

Sharon Blain / collection Transcend

Mikel Luzea / collection Art

Reds Hair & Beauty / collection Reds Mens

Petra Mechurová / collection Day After

Felicitas / collection Suite Bob

Mikel Luzea / collection Scene

Petra Mechurová / collection Architect

Petra Mechurová / collection Black Window

Mark Leeson / collection Body & Mind

Petra Mechurová / collection Bloom

Petra Mechurová / collection Stargate

Mark Leeson / collection Colour

Gym Grooming / collection Gentlemen's

Lisa Shepherd / collection Candy Stripe

Trevor Sorbie / collection Love

Petra Mechurová / collection Diabolique

Jacques Fourcade / collection Coiffure

Mark Leeson / collection Colour

Sanrizz / collection XY Neo Geo

Reds Hair & Beauty / collection Reds Mens

Petra Mechurová / collection Metro

Petra Mechurová / collection Behind the Wheel

Anne Veck / collection French Dressing

Gym Grooming / collection Summer

Mark Leeson / collection Hair, Body and Mind

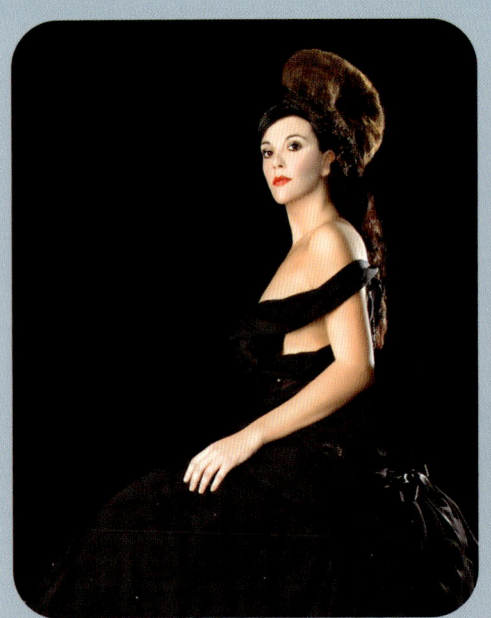

Mikel Luzea / collection Art

Barrie Stephen / collection Obsession

Sanrizz / collection XY Neo Geo

Hob Salons / collection Mens

82

Petra Mechurová / collection Behind the Wheel

Heading Out / collection Chichi Girls

Essensuals Toni & Guy / collection Vintage Vague

Kuhn the School / collection Identity of Sense

Kuhn the School / collection Stone

Patrick Cameron / collection Ladies Who Lunch

Anne Veck / collection French Dressing

Felicitas / collection Suite Bob

Jacques Fourcade / collection Coiffure

Heading Out / collection Chichi Boys

Sanrizz / collection XY Neo Geo

Essensuals Toni & Guy / collection Vintage Vague

Patrick Cameron / collection Pure

Patrick Cameron / collection Pure

Anne Veck / collection French Dressing

Sanrizz / collection XY Neo Geo

Petra Mechurová / collection Behind the Wheel

Sanrizz / collection Sephora-Electra

Richard Ward / collection Metro Chic

Patrick Cameron / collection Ladies Who Lunch

Trevor Sorbie / collection Love

Petra Mechurová / collection Metro

Sanrizz / collection XY Neo Geo

Sharon Blain / collection Long Hair

Petra Mechurová / collection Foxy

Gym Grooming / collection Summer

Michelle McKay / collection By Ishoka

Kuhn the School / collection Stones

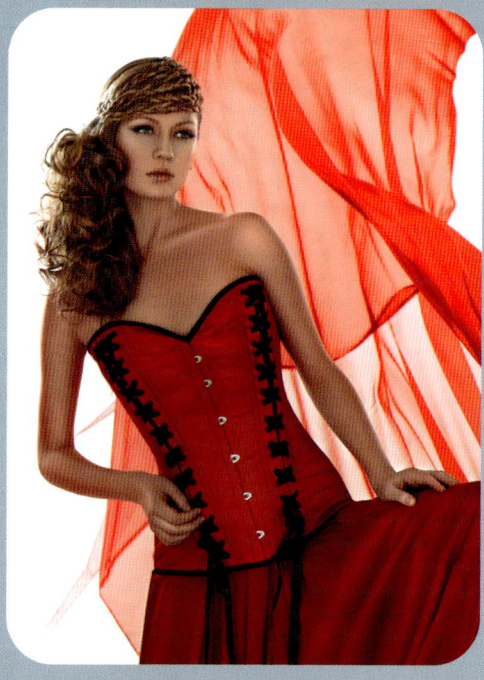

Phil Smith / collection By Gorgeous

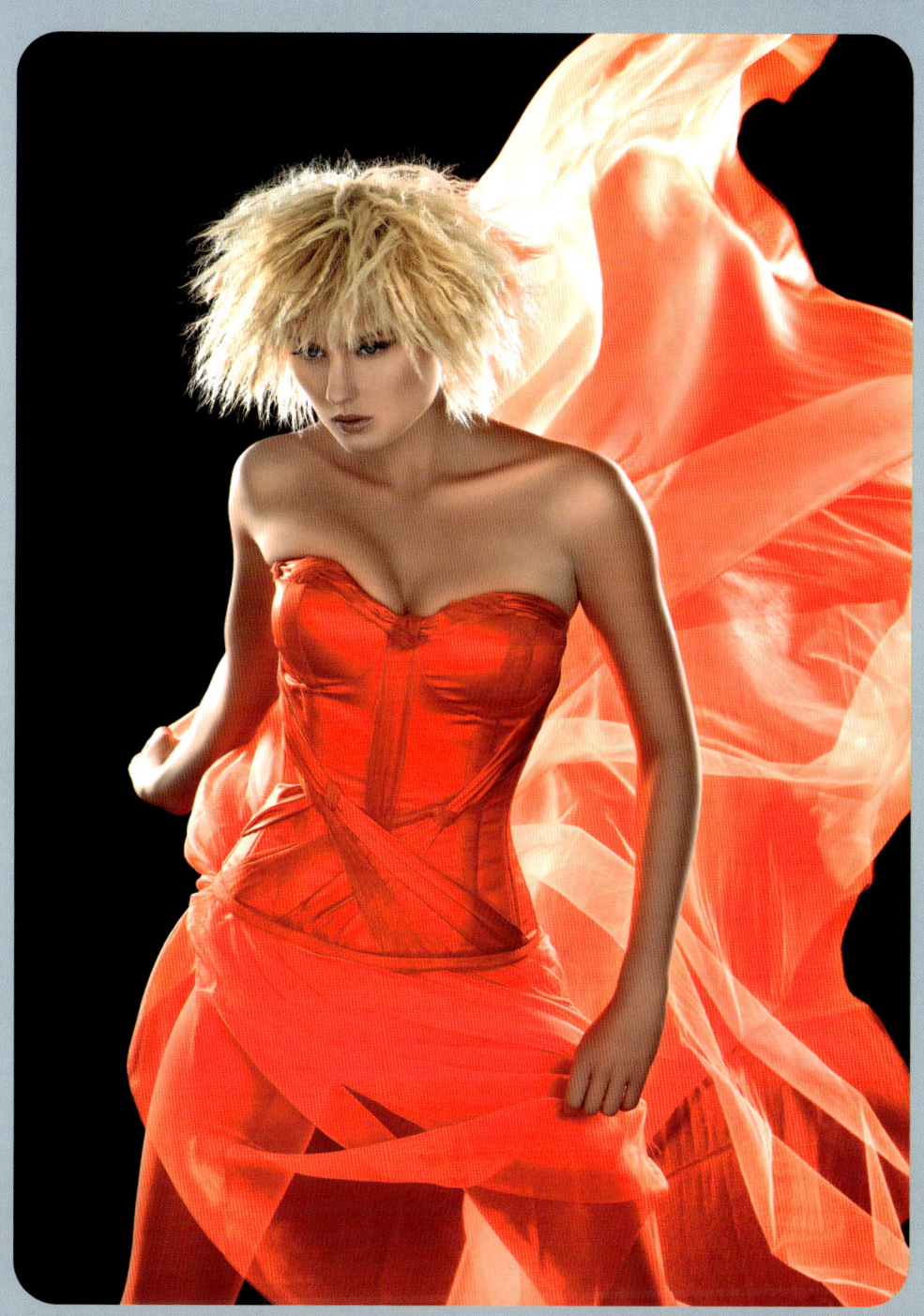

Phil Smith / collection By Gorgeous

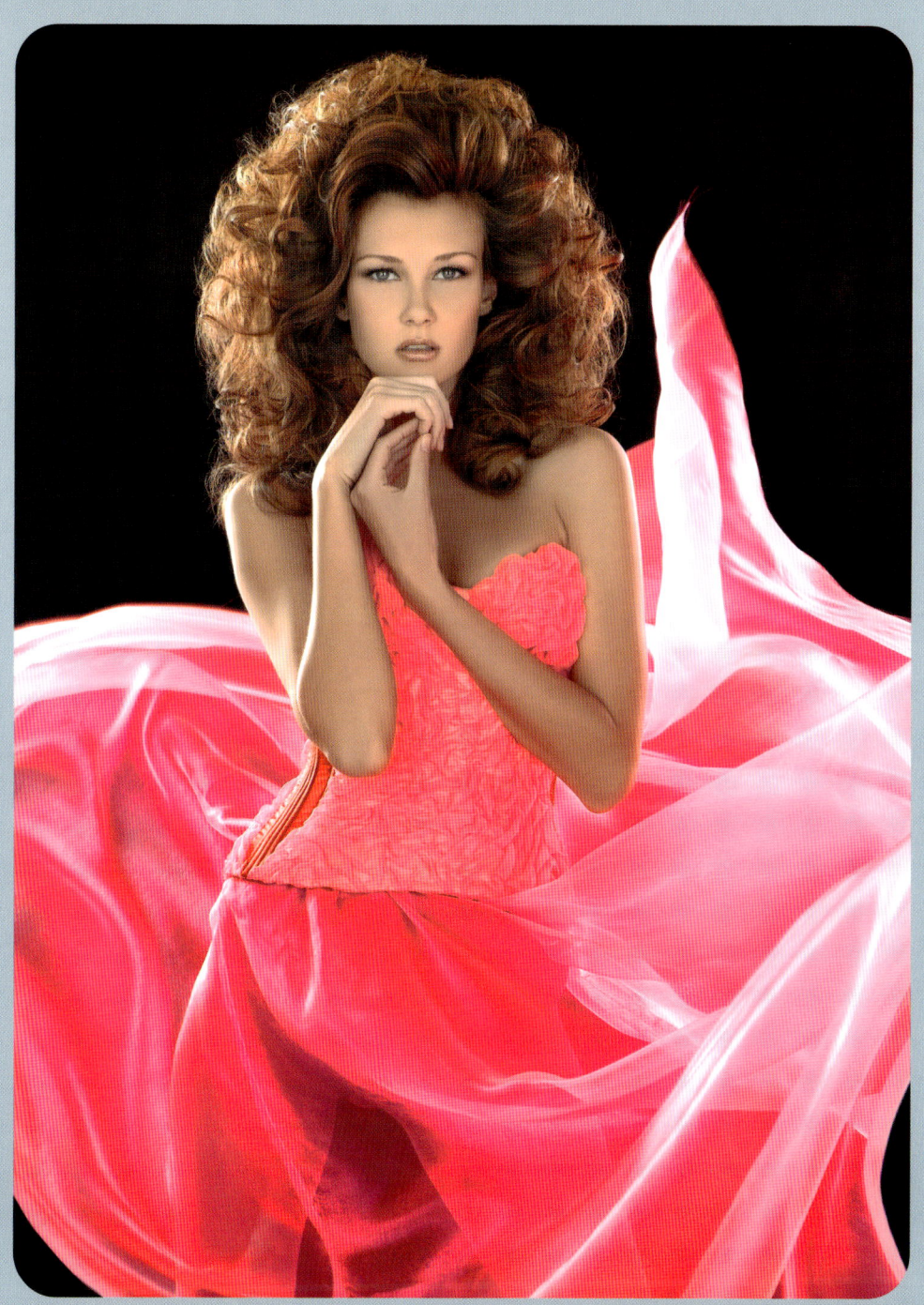

Mahogany / collection Art Cube-Esque

Michelle McKay / collection By Ishoka

Michelle McKay / collection By Ishoka

Anne Veck / collection French Dressing

Sharon Blain / collection Transcend

Petra Mechurová / collection Just Married

Petra Mechurová / collection Office

Sharon Blain / collection Long Hair

Mark Leeson / collection Hair, Body and Mind

Tarantino / collection Sweet Gourmet

Ishoka / collection Ishoka

Jacques Fourcade / collection Coiffure

Cebado / collection Casino

Alan D / collection Tommy Rocks

Petra Mechurová / collection Cocoon

Ishoka / collection Ishoka

Pierre Mollicone Paris / collection Printemps-Eté

Petra Mechurová / collection Troopers

Patrick Cameron / collection Ladies Who Lunch

Paterson SA / collection Smooth Criminal

Cebado / collection Casino

Björn Axén / collection Snake

Petra Mechurová / collection Cocoon

ALAN D
www.aland.co.uk
enquiries@aland.co.uk

ANNE VECK
www.anneveckhair.com
anne@anneveckhair.com

BARRIE STEPHEN
www.barriestephenhair.co.uk
salon@barriestephenhair.co.uk

BJÖRN AXÉN
www.axens.se
info@bjornaxen.se

CEBADO
www.cebado.es
cebado@cebado.es

TONI & GUY
www.tonyandguy.com
media@tonyandguy.co.uk

FELICITAS
www.felicitashair.com
felicitas@felicitashair.com

GYM GROOMING
www.gymgrooming.com
sales@christopherphilip.com

HEADING OUT
www.headingout.com.au
pr@headingout.com.au

HOB SALONS
www.hobsalons.com
katie@hobsalons.com

ISHOKA
www.ishokahairandbeauty.com
alison@ajc.demon.co.uk

JACQUES FOURCADE
www.jacquesfourcade.com
sales@christopherphilip.com

KUHN THE SCHOOL
www.team-kuhn.ch
info@team-kuhn.ch

LISA SHEPHERD
www.lisashepherd.co.uk
reception@lisashepherd.co.uk

MAHOGANY
www.mahoganyhair.co.uk
lottie@mahoganyhair.co.uk

THE HAIRDRESSERS

MARK LEESON
www.markleeson.co.uk
info@markleeson.co.uk

MICHELLE MCKAY
www.ishokahairandbeauty.com
alison@ajc.demon.co.uk

MIKEL LUZEA
www.mikel-luzea.com
citacentro@mikel-luzea.com

PATERSON SA
www.psahair.com
joinnewsletter@psahair.com

PATRICK CAMERON
www.patrick-cameron.com
marco@patrick-cameron.com

PETRA MECHUROVÁ
www.mechurova.cz
salon@petra.mechurova.cz

PHIL SMITH
www.philsmithhair.com
info@philsmithhair.com

PIERRE MOLLICONE PARIS
www.pierremollicone.com

REDS HAIR & BEAUTY
www.redshairandbeauty.com
info@redshairandbeauty.com

RICHARD WARD
www.richardward.co.uk
info@richardward.co.uk

TARANTINO
www.clude-tarantino.com
info@clude-tarantino.com

TREVOR SORBIE
www.trevorsorbie.com
info@trevorsorbie.com

SANRIZZ
www.sanrizz.co.uk
info@sanrizz.co.uk

SHARON BLAIN
www.sharonblain.com
info@sharonblain.com